10.14

SHRUBLANDS

David Burnie

Steck-Vaughn Company

First published 2003 by Raintree Steck-Vaughn Publishers,
an imprint of Steck-Vaughn Company.
Copyright © 2003 The Brown Reference Group plc

Library of Congress Cataloging-in-Publication Data

Burnie, David.
   Shrublands / David Burnie.
      p. cm. -- (Biomes atlases)
   Summary: A comprehensive look at the shrubland biome, describing the climate,
plants, animals, people, and future of these areas, and providing detailed views of some
major shrubland regions.
   Includes bibliographical references.
   ISBN 0-7398-5514-X
   1. Shrubland ecology--Juvenile literature. 2. Shrubland ecology--Maps--Juvenile
literature. [1. Shrublands. 2. Shrubland ecology. 3. Ecology.] I. Title. II. Series.

QH541.5.S55 B87 2003
577.3'8--dc21

                                                           2002068093

Printed in Singapore. Bound in the United States.
1 2 3 4 5 6 7 8 9 0 LB 07 06 05 04 03 02

The Brown Reference Group plc
Project Editor: Ben Morgan
Deputy Editor: Dr. Rob Houston
Consultant: Prof. David Mabberley, Honorary
      Research Associate, Royal Botanic
      Gardens, Sydney, Australia
Designer: Reg Cox
Cartographers: Mark Walker and
      Darren Awuah
Picture Researcher: Clare Newman
Indexer: Kay Ollerenshaw
Managing Editor: Bridget Giles
Design Manager: Lynne Ross
Production: Matt Weyland

Raintree Steck-Vaughn
Editor: Walter Kossmann
Production Manager: Brian Suderski

Front cover: Fynbos shrubland with protea
amd heath in foreground, Western
Cape Province, South Africa.
Inset: Provence cricket, heathland, England.

Title page: King protea, Western Cape
Province, South Africa.

The acknowledgments on p. 64 form
part of this copyright page.

About this Book

The introductory pages of this book describe the biomes of the world and then the shrubland biome. The five main chapters look at different aspects of shrublands: climate, plants, animals, people, and future. Between the chapters are detailed maps that focus on major shrubland regions. The map pages are shown in the contents in italics, *like this*.

Throughout the book you'll also find boxed stories or fact files about shrublands. The icons here show what the boxes are about. At the end of the book is a glossary, which explains what all the difficult words mean. After the glossary is a list of books and websites for further research and an index, allowing you to locate subjects anywhere in the book.

 Climate

 People

 Plants

 Future

 Animals

 Facts

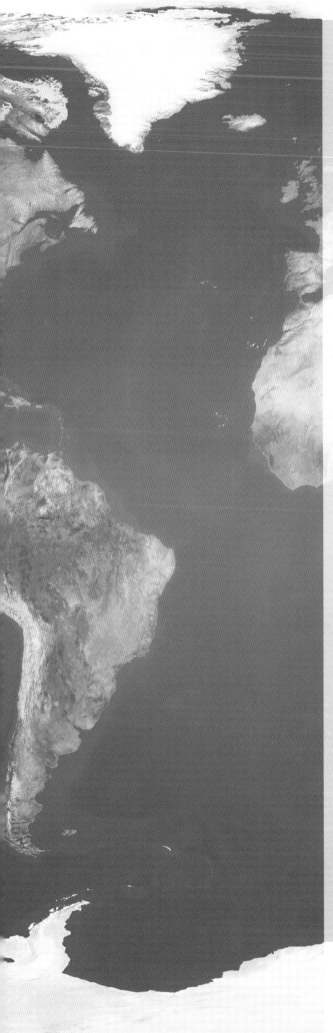

Contents

Biomes of the World

Biologists divide the living world into major zones named biomes. Each biome has its own distinctive climate, plants, and animals.

Desert is the driest biome. There are hot deserts and cold ones.

Taiga is made up of conifer trees that can survive freezing winters.

If you were to walk all the way from the north of Canada to the Amazon rain forest, you'd notice the wilderness changing dramatically along the way.

Northern Canada is a freezing and barren place without trees, where only tiny brownish-green plants can survive in the icy ground. But trudge south for long enough and you enter a magical world of conifer forests, where moose, caribou, and wolves live. After several weeks, the conifers give out, and you reach the grass-covered prairies of the central United States. The farther south you go, the drier the land gets and the hotter the sun feels, until you find yourself hiking through a cactus-filled desert. But once you reach southern Mexico, the cacti start to disappear, and strange tropical trees begin to take their place. Here, the muggy air is filled with the calls of exotic birds and the drone of tropical insects. Finally, in Colombia you cross the Andes mountain range—whose chilly peaks remind you a little of your starting point—and descend into the dense, swampy jungles of the Amazon rain forest.

Scientists have a special name for the different regions—such as desert, tropical rain forest, and prairie—that you'd pass through on such a journey. They call them biomes. Everywhere on Earth can be classified as being in one biome or another, and the same biome often appears in lots of

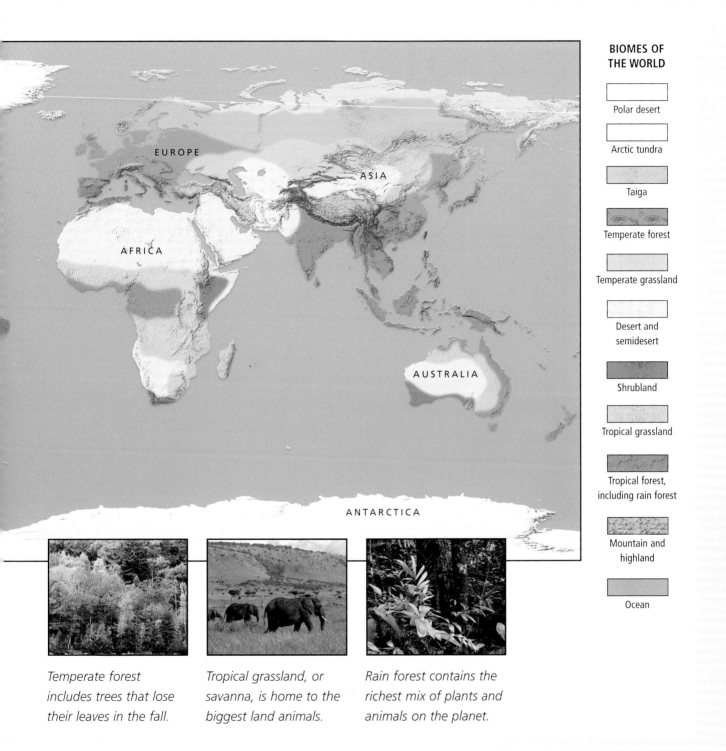

BIOMES OF
THE WORLD

Polar desert

Arctic tundra

Taiga

Temperate forest

Temperate grassland

Desert and
semidesert

Shrubland

Tropical grassland

Tropical forest,
including rain forest

Mountain and
highland

Ocean

EUROPE

ASIA

AFRICA

AUSTRALIA

ANTARCTICA

*Temperate forest
includes trees that lose
their leaves in the fall.*

*Tropical grassland, or
savanna, is home to the
biggest land animals.*

*Rain forest contains the
richest mix of plants and
animals on the planet.*

different places. For instance, there are areas of rain forest as far apart as Brazil, Africa, and Southeast Asia. Although the plants and animals that inhabit these forests are different, they live in similar ways. Likewise, the prairies of North America are part of the grassland biome, which also occurs in China, Australia, and Argentina. Wherever there are grasslands, there are grazing animals that feed on the grass, as well as large carnivores that hunt and kill the grazers.

The map on this page shows how the world's major biomes fit together to make up the biosphere—the zone of life on Earth.

Shrublands of the World

Tougher than trees and often much better armed, shrubs form the main plant cover in some widely scattered parts of the world.

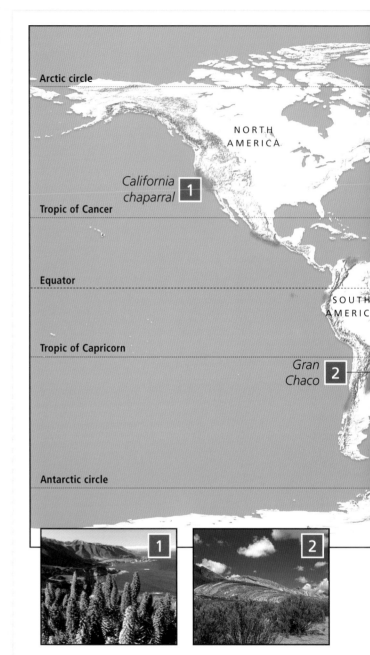

The California chaparral shrubs survive intense and regular wildfires.

The Gran Chaco in South America is thorny, dry, and impenetrable.

Shrubs occupy an in-between slot in the world of plant life. Like trees they have woody stems, but unlike trees they rarely grow more than a few feet tall. Shrubland plants grow in places where the climate is too dry for trees but still moist enough to prevent desert from taking hold.

Shrub, Scrub, or Bush?

Compared to some biomes, shrubland has a confusing variety of names. Many experts call it scrub or scrubland, while in Australia it is often known simply as the bush.

In North America, the shrubland on the California coast contains a rich variety of plants. This kind of shrubland is known as chaparral, while in South America a similar kind of shrubland is called chaco or matorral. If you travel eastward, beyond the California chaparral, the landscape becomes drier still. Chaparral gives way to the semidesert of the Great Basin, where sagebrush scrub stretches for mile after mile to the Rocky Mountains, creating scenery that is familiar the world over as the backdrop to westerns.

On the other side of the Atlantic Ocean, around the shores of the Mediterranean, shrubland hugs the coast and the hillsides. In one type of shrubland, called maquis, the

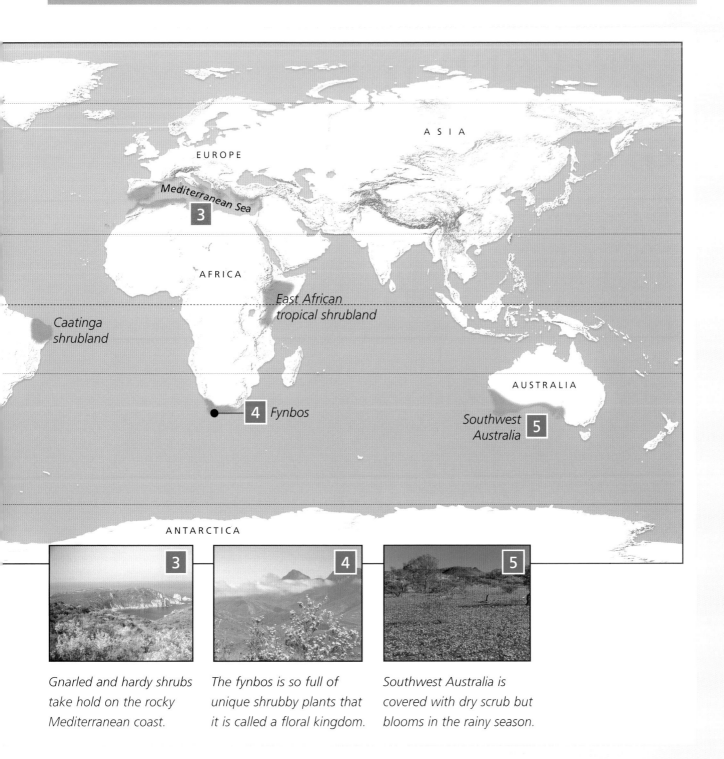

ASIA

EUROPE

Mediterranean Sea

3

AFRICA

East African
tropical shrubland

Caatinga
shrubland

4 Fynbos

AUSTRALIA

Southwest
Australia 5

ANTARCTICA

3

4

5

Gnarled and hardy shrubs take hold on the rocky Mediterranean coast.

The fynbos is so full of unique shrubby plants that it is called a floral kingdom.

Southwest Australia is covered with dry scrub but blooms in the rainy season.

shrubs grow to more than head height, making them a good refuge for animals. In drier parts of the Mediterranean, maquis is replaced by a kind of shrubland called garigue. Its shrubs are small, stunted, and scattered, with tiny leaves that are good at coping with the burning summer sun.

Shrubland grows in Australia and Africa, too. In tropical Africa, dry shrubland merges into savanna (grassland). In the far south, however, in the Cape region, it forms a dense green carpet. Called fynbos, this form of shrubland is made up of the most concentrated variety of plants on Earth.

California Chaparral

The backdrop to dozens of Hollywood films, chaparral is typical of southern California. Large areas have been cleared, but on the mountains along the coast, lots of chaparral remains almost untouched.

Scrub Oaks

If you are used to thinking of oaks as trees, the oaks of California's chaparral could come as a surprise. These oaks often have prickly leaves, and are often less than 6 feet (1.8 m) tall even when fully grown. They may not look like the tall oaks of New England and Europe, but their acorns make it easy to see through their disguise. The California scrub oak is one of the most prevalent of the chaparral's shrubby trees. Spanish colonists called it *chaparro*, which is how the chaparral got its name.

1. Sierra Nevada
California's highest mountains prevent moisture from reaching the Great Basin, creating the climate for dry sagebrush scrub.

2. San Francisco
This city marks the northern limit of the chaparral.

3. Central Valley
Formerly an area of grassland and shrubland; now a major fruit-growing region.

4. Coast Ranges
The rare California condor soars over the montane chaparral that grows on these mountains.

5. Angeles National Forest
Chaparral-covered foothills lead to pine-clad summits.

6. Santa Monica Mountains
A national recreation area where visitors can hike, bike, and enjoy the wildflowers.

7. Los Angeles
This major city lies in the heart of California's shrublands.

8. Channel Islands
Rugged islands that have unique animals such as the island night lizard and the Santa Catalina shrew.

9. Santa Catalina Island
On this island, conservationists are restoring chaparral by removing introduced animals.

10. Torrey Pines State Reserve
The rare torrey pine grows in only one place on the mainland: a patch within this reserve 2 square miles (5 sq km) in area. The pine also lives on Santa Rosa Island.

11. Baja California
The chaparral extends into the north of this peninsula. Prickly pears and yuccas become more common in the drier south.

Lupins burst into flower on the California coast in spring.

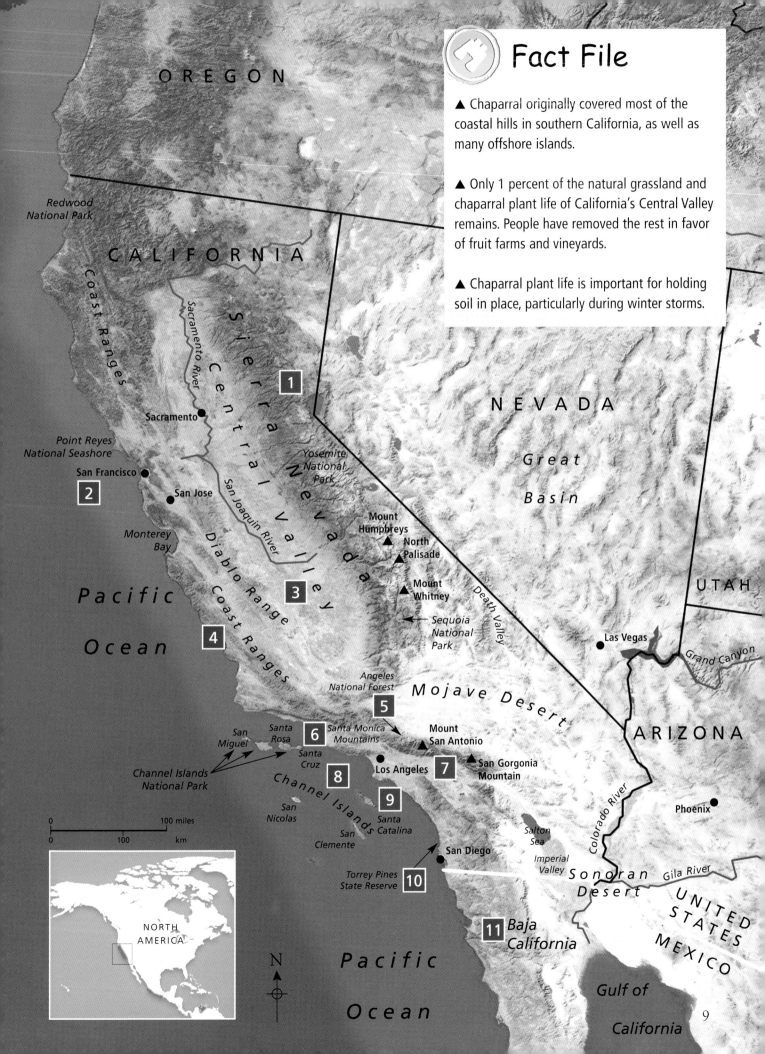

OREGON

CALIFORNIA

Redwood
National Park

Coast Ranges

Sacramento River

Sierra Nevada

Central Valley

1

Sacramento

Point Reyes
National Seashore

San Francisco

2

San Jose

Monterey
Bay

San Joaquin River

Diablo Range

3

Coast Ranges

Pacific

4

Ocean

Yosemite
National
Park

Mount
Humphreys ▲ ▲ North
Palisade

▲ Mount
Whitney

Death Valley

→ Sequoia
National
Park

NEVADA

Great

Basin

UTAH

Las Vegas

Grand Canyon

Mojave Desert

Angeles
National Forest

5

San
Miguel

Santa
Rosa

6

Santa Monica →
Mountains

Channel Islands
National Park

Santa
Cruz

8

Channel Islands

9

San
Nicolas

Santa
Catalina

San
Clemente

Mount
San Antonio ▲

Los Angeles

7

▲ San Gorgonia
Mountain

ARIZONA

Colorado River

Salton
Sea

Phoenix

San Diego

Imperial
Valley

Sonoran

Gila River

Torrey Pines
State Reserve

10

11 Baja
California

Desert

UNITED
STATES

MEXICO

0   100 miles

0   100
        km

NORTH
AMERICA

N

Pacific

Ocean

Gulf of

California

▲ Chaparral originally covered most of the coastal hills in southern California, as well as many offshore islands.

▲ Only 1 percent of the natural grassland and chaparral plant life of California's Central Valley remains. People have removed the rest in favor of fruit farms and vineyards.

▲ Chaparral plant life is important for holding soil in place, particularly during winter storms.

Shrubland Climates

Most of the world's shrublands have one thing in common: They normally grow where water is scarce for several months each year.

If you imagine being burned by strong sunshine and battered by dust-laden winds, you will have an idea what the shrubland climate is often like. However, unlike deserts, shrublands are not always dry. Although some shrublands receive less than 8 inches (200 mm) of rain a year, it is unevenly spread, and a lot of rain might arrive within a short time. Meanwhile, the rest of the year might be endlessly dry. The unevenness of the rainfall makes it hard for trees to survive.

Mediterranean Climate

Most of the world's shrublands are on the west coast of continents, sandwiched between regions where it is always hot and regions where winters are cold. In shrubland regions, much of the year's rain falls in winter, and although it can get cold, hard frosts are rare. When spring arrives, the temperature quickly climbs, and by the time summer sets in, weeks can go by with hardly a cloud in the sky. At the height of summer, temperatures sometimes reach more than 100°F (38°C), leaving dead plant matter tinder dry.

This mixture of moist winters and dry summers is known

Fire!

In shrublands, fires are a natural fact of life. Triggered by lightning, they are often fanned by summer winds, and they can move faster than a person can run. During these fires, shrubs are left charred and blackened, but when the fire has passed, the shrubs can resprout from the ground. The trees of shrubland regions are often killed by the heat, so occasional fires help stop shrubland from turning into forest. These days, fires are also started by campfires and cigarettes. The more frequent blazes make it even harder for trees to survive.

as a Mediterranean climate, but the Mediterranean region is not the only place where it occurs. Across the world, from California and Chile to South Africa and western Australia, similar conditions encourage similar shrubland plants. The climate is ideal for grapevines, which is why so many of the world's wines come from these parts of the world.

Wind and Fire

Warmth and rainwater are not the only things that shape life in places with Mediterranean climates. Another important factor is the wind. In summer, a daytime breeze often blows onto the land from the sea, helping to take the edge off the heat. But sometimes the wind swings around and blows from inland, and when this happens, conditions can quickly change.

This is exactly what occurs in southern California, when the Santa Ana wind blows. It brings hot dusty air from the desert, and it sends temperatures shooting up. Because the Santa Ana wind is hot and bone dry, it can turn sparks into major scrub and forest fires. Shrubland plants have their own ways of coping with this threat, and once the fire is over, most of them recover. But for people, these fires are much more of a problem— particularly when their homes stand in the path of the flames.

In the Mediterranean region a similar wind, called the sirocco, sometimes blows northward out of Africa. It brings the same kind of stifling heat and often carries sand from the Sahara, dropping it hundreds of miles away. Mediterranean wildlife also has to deal with cold winter winds, such as the mistral, which blows down from the north.

Nature's Thermometer

The olive tree thrives in the Mediterranean climate. The distribution of olive trees reliably shows us which parts of the world have a climate similar to the Mediterranean. Olive trees like lots of hot sunshine in the summer, but they will not grow in places where the average winter temperature drops below 37.5°F (3°C). Even a few hours of frost can kill them. The olive tree originally came from the eastern Mediterranean, but its fruit and oil are so useful that farmers now grow it in places as far apart as California and Australia.

Climographs

Each place in the world has its own pattern of weather. The typical pattern of weather over a year in one place is called the place's climate. We can sum up a place's climate on a climograph, such as the one shown here for St. Louis. The letters along the bottom are the months of the year. The numbers on the left and the small bars show rainfall, and the numbers on the right and the curvy line show temperature. You can see at a glance that St. Louis is hottest in July, but December is the driest month.

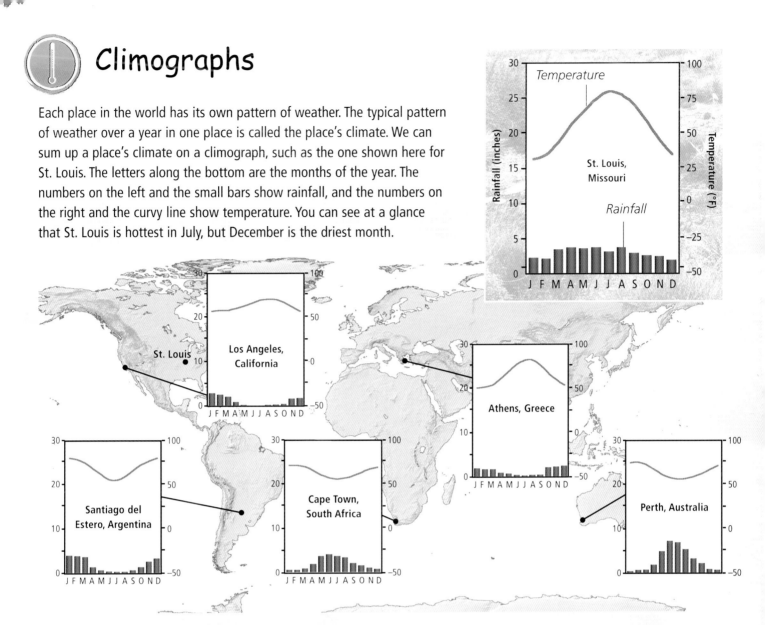

When the mistral is blowing, the temperature can fall to near freezing, spelling danger to animals and plants that cannot cope with frost. The olive tree is one of these vulnerable species: Every few years, the cold wipes out large numbers of them.

Storms and Salt

On the fringes of deserts, the climate is drier than the typical Mediterranean climate, and shrubs fight a constant battle to stay alive. A tiny amount of extra moisture can make all the difference. Many desert-edge shrubs survive in dry riverbeds, where flash floods occur after sudden storms. Between these floods, there is no sign of water on the surface, but water collects underground, beneath the dry riverbed. The shrubs survive by soaking up this leftover moisture.

When rain does fall in dry shrublands, it can create problems. It can run off the dry ground instead of soaking in, forming sudden floods. These floods often dissolve salt from the soil and carry it downhill. Once a storm has passed and the sun comes out, pools and puddles left by the flood quickly dry up, leaving their salt behind. The leftover salt makes the ground sparkle and feel crunchy underfoot, and it spells deadly danger to many plants. Salt makes it hard for plants to soak up water, and it eventually kills their roots. But some shrubs survive in salty soil.

Saltbushes on Australia's Nullarbor Plain appear gray-green because of the salt crystals on their leaves. The crystals reflect sunlight and keep the saltbushes cool.

Saltbushes, for instance, live in areas that receive their rainfall in less than a dozen sudden bursts each year.

Australia's vast Nullarbor Plain is one place where saltbushes have the ground largely to themselves. *Nullarbor* means "no tree," and as plains go, this one could hardly be plainer. It is wide open, pancake flat, and twice as big as the state of New York. Small trees do grow here, but saltbushes are the most common plants. They stretch from horizon to horizon, creating a lonely landscape crossed by a railroad that does not need to bend for 300 miles (500 km). It is the longest straight stretch of railroad in the world.

Like saltbushes in other dry shrublands, the Nullarbor's saltbushes have a way of getting rid of surplus salt. They make crystals of the salt on their leaves, which gives the leaves a gray-green color and a rough texture.

 # Beating the Heat

On the Greek island of Rhodes, summer can get too hot even for insects. Here, millions of tiger moths spend the hottest time of the year in a handful of shady valleys, where they cluster in rock crevices and over shrubs and small trees. Their black-and-white forewings camouflage them well when they are at rest, but as soon as they take off, their brilliant orange hind wings seem to flash through the air. Because the moths fly by day, they are often mistaken for butterflies.

Shrublands in the Tropics

In the tropics, the climate is usually wet enough for forest or grassland to flourish, so shrubs find themselves crowded out. But in some places, such as northeast Brazil and parts of Africa, there is a long dry season each year. In this climate, trees and even grasses may struggle to survive, so shrubs can get the upper hand. In these places, most of the rain falls at the hottest time of year—the exact opposite of the Mediterranean climate. In southern Africa, for example, July is the coolest month, because it is the middle of the southern hemisphere's winter. It is also the driest month, often with no rain at all. In January, though, the air is sticky and humid (moist), and towering thunderclouds release torrential downpours almost every afternoon.

This switch between wet and dry times has some far-reaching effects. During the wet season, shrubs are covered with leaves, so even large animals are well hidden. But during the dry

In the stressful, dry climate of east Africa's shrublands, plants can't put up with too many browsing animals. The shrubs defend themselves with thorns, but the black rhino is tough enough to eat them.

In Baja California, the climate is drier than the Mediterranean climate of California. There are more succulent (fleshy) plants like the prickly pear cactus.

when water holes become very busy, as animals arrive from far and wide to take a much-needed drink.

Africa has more large plant-eaters than anywhere else on Earth, so it's not surprising that many shrubs and small trees have spines and thorns for self-defense. During the dry season, their bare branches are like strands of barbed wire, and anything that tangles with them can take a long time to work itself free.

Coastal Shrubland

Even in places with plenty of rain, climate can sometimes give shrubs the edge over trees. This often happens on cold, windswept coasts, where trees would be uprooted and blown away. This kind of environment is common around the shores of northern Germany and Denmark, and on the western shores of the British Isles. Storm-force winds can lash these coasts with salt-laden spray at speeds of more than 65 mph (103 km/h). Winds this fast can knock people off their feet, but shrubs like gorse and buckthorn are small and tough enough to stay in place.

These coastal shrubs are like natural windbreakers. They create a sheltered microclimate near the ground. Tucked away inside them, animals can sit out the storm, waiting until it is safe to venture outside.

season, many of the shrubs lose their foliage, and the grass between them dies down. This is the best time to watch wildlife, because there is much less cover and far fewer places for animals to hide. It is also the time of year

The Welsh coast doesn't have a Mediterranean climate. Shrubland develops here because trees can't grow in the wind and salty spray. Tough gorse and heather grow in their place.

These seaside stowaways include small birds, small mammals, and even delicate animals like butterflies, which flit over shrubs and coastal grass when calm weather returns. Because the sea breeze almost always blows from the same direction, these shrubs are often lopsided, with their twigs and branches pointing inland.

Guilty Goats

Climate is not the only thing that can create or destroy shrublands: humans can also play a part. Sometimes the changes people make are easy to see. For example, shrublands are plowed up and turned into fields. But in some parts of the world, the changes occurred so long ago that it is not easy to work out what happened. To unravel this hidden history, scientists examine today's plant cover and climate. They then compare it with what they would expect to see if the land had been left truly wild. This research shows that some shrubland regions are not nearly as natural as they seem.

One of the biggest shrubland areas, around the Mediterranean Sea, probably formed when people began to farm the land and cut down many of the trees. Some 10,000 years ago, the Mediterranean area was thickly forested, and forest stretched down to the shore. But as farming expanded, more and more spaces were opened up, so that crops could be grown and animals fed. Once the forest had been felled, goats nibbled away at young saplings and stopped the forest from growing back. The story of the Mediterranean shows that people, as well as climate, have helped create the shrublands that we see today.

This ancient Roman plate shows that people and their goats have been living in the shrubland biome of the Mediterranean region for thousands of years.

From Forest to Chaparral

At Rancho La Brea in California, the remains of thousands of prehistoric animals have been found in natural pools of oily tar. The animals include mammoths, giant ground sloths, and saber-toothed tigers, all of which fell into the tar by accident, mistaking it for solid ground. These giant mammals lived during the last ice age, when southern California was covered by forest. They died out during the time when humans spread into North America, between 20,000 and 12,000 years ago. This was also a time when the climate warmed at the end of the Ice Age, and the biomes of North America moved and changed. The widespread forest biome in California turned to chaparral.

The Gran Chaco

Straddling Argentina, Bolivia, and Paraguay, the Gran Chaco is one of the harshest areas of shrubland in the world. Fierce summer heat, thorny scrub, and poisonous snakes make this a difficult place to live.

Above right: The Gran Chaco is full of poisonous snakes, but among the most dangerous is a viper called the urutu. *Human victims of its bites develop blisters and bleed from their nose and gums.*

Below: The High Chaco of Argentina looks barren and unpromising, but ten different types of armadillo, including the pink fairy armadillo, live there.

1. Amboro National Park
The size of Delaware, this park includes Amazon rain forest and Andean foothills besides the northernmost chaco. Its animals include jaguars, margays, and armadillos.

2. Mato Grosso Plateau
The plateau is a sweep of high ground covered with a mosaic of grassland and shrubland.

3. Pantanal
A vast expanse of seasonal wetland, legendary for its rich wildlife, including 600 species of birds.

4. Defenders of the Chaco National Park
This dry area of impenetrable thorn-tree forest is a refuge for giant anteaters and the chacoan peccary, a hoofed piglike animal that lives nowhere else in the world.

5. High Chaco
The mountainous High Chaco, the western edge of the Gran Chaco, is dense thorn forest.

6. Queñoa Forest
The High Chaco extends up into the Andes mountains, where the scrubby queñoa trees of Bolivia are the world's highest living trees.

7. Filadelfia
A remote town in the heart of the Paraguayan chaco, founded by members of a German-speaking religious community called the Mennonites.

8. Paraguay River
This major river marks the Gran Chaco's eastern edge.

9. Low Chaco
The eastern edge of the Gran Chaco is made up of grassland with scattered shrubs and trees.

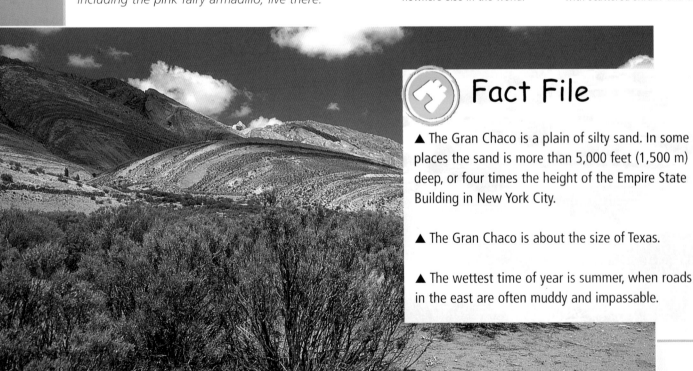

Fact File

▲ The Gran Chaco is a plain of silty sand. In some places the sand is more than 5,000 feet (1,500 m) deep, or four times the height of the Empire State Building in New York City.

▲ The Gran Chaco is about the size of Texas.

▲ The wettest time of year is summer, when roads in the east are often muddy and impassable.

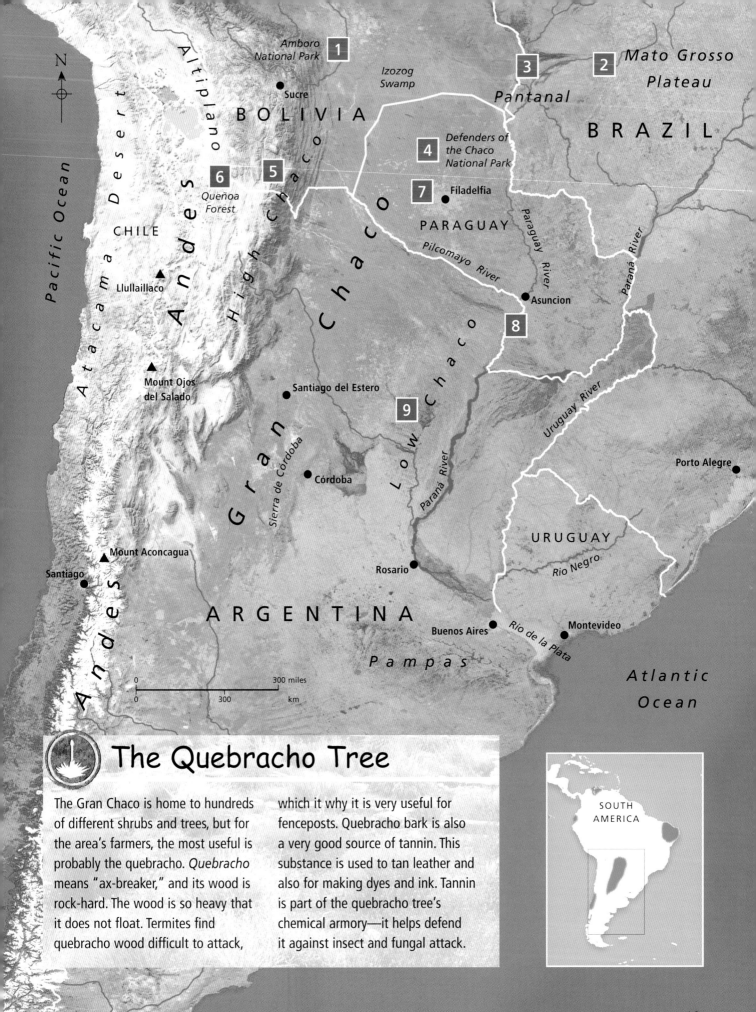

N

Pacific Ocean

Altiplano

Atacama Desert

BOLIVIA

Sucre

Izozog Swamp

[1] Amboro National Park

[3]

[2] Mato Grosso Plateau

Pantanal

BRAZIL

[6]

Queñoa Forest

[5]

High Chaco

[4] Defenders of the Chaco National Park

[7] Filadelfia

CHILE

Andes

PARAGUAY

Gran Chaco

Pilcomayo River

Paraguay River

Paraná River

Llullaillaco

Asuncion

[8]

Mount Ojos del Salado

Santiago del Estero

Low Chaco

Uruguay River

Sierra de Córdoba

[9]

Córdoba

Paraná River

Porto Alegre

URUGUAY

Mount Aconcagua

Rio Negro

Santiago

Rosario

ARGENTINA

Buenos Aires

Río de la Plata

Montevideo

Pampas

Atlantic Ocean

0 ——— 300 miles
0 ——— 300 km

SOUTH AMERICA

The Quebracho Tree

The Gran Chaco is home to hundreds of different shrubs and trees, but for the area's farmers, the most useful is probably the quebracho. *Quebracho* means "ax-breaker," and its wood is rock-hard. The wood is so heavy that it does not float. Termites find quebracho wood difficult to attack, which it why it is very useful for fenceposts. Quebracho bark is also a very good source of tannin. This substance is used to tan leather and also for making dyes and ink. Tannin is part of the quebracho tree's chemical armory—it helps defend it against insect and fungal attack.

19

Shrubland Plants

Shrubs are tough customers. Besides hot sunshine and long droughts, they have to survive hungry animals and the threat of catching fire.

Shrubs put up with damage that would kill many other plants. If they are eaten, chopped down, or even set on fire, most of them simply grow back.

Rebirth from the Ashes

One of the best places to see how shrubs bounce back is in the interior of southern Australia, where mallee shrubland covers thousands of square miles. Mallees are eucalyptuses or gum trees, but instead of growing tall and lean, like most eucalyptuses, they are usually small, with gnarled and twisted stems. They don't win any prizes for beauty, but they are experts at staying alive.

As a mallee shrub grows, it drops dead leaves and old branches on the ground. Mixed with dry grass, and baked by the sun, they make the perfect recipe for a fire. A flash of lightning or a discarded cigarette is all it takes to set this fuel on fire, and within hours, thousands of acres can be ablaze.

In the Stirling Range of southwest Australia, fresh green shoots burst out of the blackened trunks of grass trees and mallee shrubs after a bushfire.

The plant life in South Africa's fynbos shrubland is as spectacular as it is diverse. The king protea is crowned by gigantic blooms that are pollinated (fertilized) by Cape sugarbirds.

For small animals, such as crickets and lizards, these blazes are a deadly danger. Even birds can be threatened when the mallees burst into flames. But once the fire has passed, the shrubland stages an incredible recovery. Within a few weeks, the charred trunks start to sprout new stems and leaves. The cleared ground between the shrubs begins to turn green with plants springing from previously dormant (inactive) seeds. Because all the dead wood and leaves have been burned away, years pass before a serious fire can strike again.

Mallees can stage a miraculous comeback because each one has a stockpile of water and food. It is hidden in a swollen root called a lignotuber, which is safely buried underground. Lignotubers can be as big as wheelbarrows, and they contain all that mallees need to get going after a disaster.

Scents in the Air

Mallees are 100 percent Australian, and you won't find them anywhere else. In the same way, many other shrubland plants live in just one part of the world. For example, papery-petaled shrubs called cistus grow only around the Mediterranean, while greasewood lives only in California's chaparral. But despite looking different, and living far apart, shrubs like these share some features that allow them to live in the same conditions.

Grass Trees

In western Australia, plants called grass trees flower only after a fire. They look like small palm trees topped by a tuft of grasslike leaves. When a fire strikes, the leaves soon burn away, and in bad fires, the trunks themselves can burn almost to the ground. But within a few weeks, new leaves sprout, followed by flowers. Grass trees can grow up to 30 feet (10 m) tall, and their trunks are usually black and covered with soot. Their young leaves are sweet and succulent, and for Australia's aboriginal people, they were once a useful source of food.

One of these features can't be seen. You can smell it, though, if you brush past a shrub or rub some of its leaves. If you are in a place with a Mediterranean-type climate, the chances are that an aromatic odor fills the air. This smell comes from oils in the leaves, which evaporate (turn to vapor) when the leaves are touched or bruised.

To human noses, some of these oily smells are not nice. Others, for example those of lavender and sage, are much more pleasant, which is why these plants are used for making perfumes or for flavoring food. But these plant oils have not evolved for our benefit—shrubs use them for protection. Oils prevent leaves from losing too much water when they are heated by sunshine. This is an essential feature for life where summers are hot and long. To back up this water-saving system, oily leaves often have a leathery surface or a covering of microscopic hairs. A leathery surface keeps water in, while hairs work like sunshades, helping to keep the leaf cool. Another way shrubs beat the heat is to keep their leaves small. Greasewood has leaves like small pine needles, making it very good at surviving on hot windswept ground.

Oils also discourage hungry plant eaters, because oily leaves are difficult to digest. This smelly defense explains why few animals can stomach the leaves of Australia's mallees or of many other shrubs that grow where it is dry. In fact, oily plants often benefit when farm animals arrive on the scene: Cattle or goats eat all the tastier plants, leaving more room for the oily plants to spread.

The Summer Sleepers
After several months of drought, shrubs often look parched and dusty, and the ground between them seems bare. But beneath the surface, a host of plants lie hidden, waiting for the right moment to grow. These are the shrubland's summer sleepers—plants that

After a hot summer in Africa's dry shrubland, the only sign of life from shrubs such as the impala lily is a display of flowers. It will grow its leaves again in spring.

disappear during the hottest time of the year. In summer, the plants live on their private stores of food and water, which they keep underground, usually inside swollen roots.

Sea squill of southern Europe is one of the biggest of these sleeping plants. Its swollen root is a bulb almost as big as a football, and it is packed with poison that helps keep hungry animals at bay. During winter, the plant has a cluster of succulent (fleshy), shiny leaves, but when spring arrives, they slowly die away. At the height of summer, the leaves

Some wasps help the fig plant by pollinating its tiny flowers when they crawl into a fig to lay their eggs. This wasp cheats: it uses a long tube on its abdomen, called an ovipositor, to insert eggs directly into the fig.

abdomen

ovipositor

have completely disappeared, and the plant is deep in its summer rest. But when summer nears its end, the bulb comes back to life, and the plant bursts into flower.

Fall flowering is a common feature of dry shrubland, but an even more spectacular flowering takes place in spring. This is the time when thousands of small plants rush to reproduce, before the hot weather bakes their leaves. They include tulips, lilies, irises, and crocuses, all of which have fleshy roots, bulbs, or tubers that store food. Some orchids that grow from tubers also join the spring bloom. If conditions get really difficult, some can survive without sprouting for several years. In western Australia, one species of shrubland orchid spends almost its entire life underground. A sharp-eyed farmer discovered

it in 1928, while he was plowing. Only the flowers of this fascinating plant, the western underground orchid, appear at ground level, to be pollinated by termites.

 ## Chemical Warfare

Shrubland plants can be as ruthless as animals in defending their own patch of ground. One way they do this is by producing poisonous chemicals, which seep through the soil and prevent other plants from growing nearby.

In the American west, sagebrush (below) is an expert at this kind of chemical warfare. Rings of bare soil often surround mature sagebrush plants. These rings are the equivalent of no man's land, and they give sagebrush extra room to grow.

Visitors on the Wing

When plants are growing, they need to keep animals away from their leaves. But once they start flowering, they often need animal help to spread their pollen and seeds. For shrubland plants, attracting the right kind of visitors at the right time is essential.

Few shrubs are as particular as the edible fig tree, which grows wild around the Mediterranean. The figs—the fleshy parts that people sell in fruit markets—are not really fruit, but hollow swellings packed with tiny flowers. Each fig has a concealed entrance at its tip, which is the way in for the female fig wasp—a flying insect not much larger than a flea. The wasp pollinates the fig's flowers, and in return, the fig acts as a nursery for the wasp's young.

The female wasp has to crawl along a narrow passage leading inside the fig. During this journey, she often loses her feelers or wings. As she clambers about, choosing the

These colors reflect the richness (number of different species) of plant life. Intense pinks and reds show the places with the most plant species. They include mountain ranges, where several biomes are squashed together. They also include patches of rich tropical rain forest in the Congo and Borneo.

The other hot spots of plant richness are shrublands, such as southwest Australia and the fynbos. So why are shrublands filled with some of the most diverse mixtures of plants?

Shrubland often has a canopy of tall shrubs, with a layer of undergrowth, so there is room for more types of plants than in grassland. A shrubland canopy, however, is broken and patchy, and it lets plenty of light through for different plants to crowd in below. This makes shrubland different from temperate (cool) forests, where a few dominant species of tree form a dense canopy and stop many other types of plant from growing. Even in the Mediterranean, the blue area on the map shows there are more plant species than in the green temperate forest regions nearby.

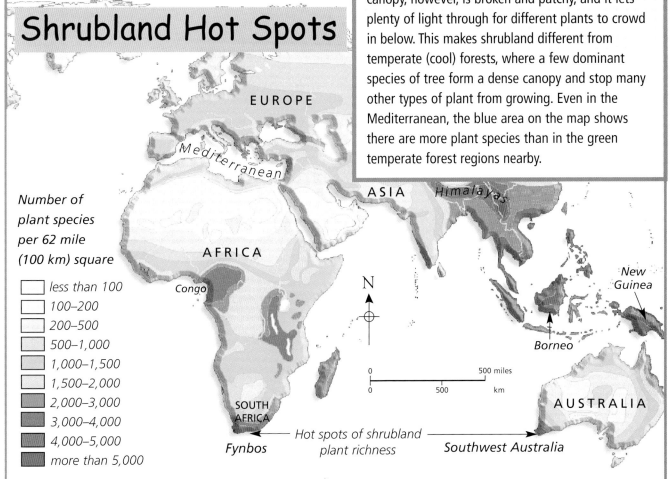

Shrubland Hot Spots

Number of plant species per 62 mile (100 km) square

- less than 100
- 100–200
- 200–500
- 500–1,000
- 1,000–1,500
- 1,500–2,000
- 2,000–3,000
- 3,000–4,000
- 4,000–5,000
- more than 5,000

EUROPE

Mediterranean

ASIA   Himalayas

AFRICA

Congo

New Guinea

Borneo

N

0   500 miles
0   500   km

SOUTH AFRICA

AUSTRALIA

Fynbos

Hot spots of shrubland plant richness

Southwest Australia

Heathers

From Scandinavia, through the Mediterranean (right) to South Africa, heathers are important shrubland plants. There are more than 700 different kinds, but most live in the fynbos. They all have woody stems and small leaves so they can withstand heat as well as cold. Some heathers are almost tree-sized, while others creep along close to the ground. Heather flowers provide nectar for bees, while grouse and other ground-feeding birds eat the leaves. In Europe and Africa, heather was once an important building material, used for making thatched roofs.

right spot to lay her eggs, she dusts the flowers with pollen that she is carrying. The female's work is hard and when it is over, she soon dies. A short while later, her young start to hatch, and they feed on some of the flowers. The male wasps spend their lives in the fig, but the females crawl out and fly off to find figs of their own. Once they have laid their eggs and pollinated their figs, the strange cycle is complete.

The cultivated figs that we eat have flowers too long for fig wasps to lay their eggs in. The wasps pollinate them all the same, because they mistake them for wild figs.

Bee Flowers

Fig trees depend entirely on fig wasps, but many other shrubland plants are not as fussy about which insects they attract. Bees or wasps pollinate some, while other plants attract butterflies and moths. Bee-pollinated shrubs include hundreds of species in the pea family. Peas are easy to recognize, because many of them have yellow flowers with a built-in landing platform for bees, known as a keel. Flowers like these are the right shape for a bee to push open, but they will also open if you give them a slight squeeze.

For butterflies and moths, pea-flower nectar is often beyond reach. Butterflies cannot risk pushing and shoving their delicate bodies into flowers. Instead, they are attracted by tube-shaped flowers, which they probe with their long, slender tongues.

Butterfly-pollinated shrubs grow all over the world, but some of the most handsome kinds, called butterfly bushes or buddleias, come from South America and China. Butterfly bush nectar is packed with sugars, and it is so strong-smelling that it can lure butterflies from up to half a mile (nearly 1 km) downwind. It's small wonder that gardeners love these shrubs, which is why you can see them growing thousands of miles from their original homes.

Attracting Birds and Mammals

In shrublands north of the equator, most plants rely on insects to pollinate their flowers. But in the southern hemisphere, many shrubs attract birds instead. Because birds are much heavier than insects, their flowers have to be tougher, and they double up as a feeding station and a sturdy perch.

Distant Cousins

Proteas and banksias have a lot in common, and they belong to the same family of plants. But proteas live only in Africa, while banksias (below) are Australian. So why do these similar-looking relatives live such an enormous distance apart? Scientists now think that the ancestors of the bushes were trees of tropical rain forests that covered a giant continent called Gondwana. Around 100 million years ago, Gondwana broke into Africa, Australia, and South America, and stretches of ocean separated the common ancestors of proteas and banksias. The plants continued to evolve (change), but they did so separately on different continents. Over millions of years, both developed thick, leathery leaves and shrubby growth. Because they evolved in similar conditions in Africa and Australia, they ended up looking alike.

The king protea of South Africa is one of the most impressive of these bird-pollinated plants. It is an evergreen bush up to 6 feet (1.8 m) tall, studded with flower heads shaped like giant ice-cream cones surrounded by spiky flaps. Each flower head is made up of several hundred mini-flowers, or florets. When the king protea is in full bloom, it's a spectacular sight, which is why it is South Africa's national flower.

The king protea flowers throughout the year, and once each flower head has opened, it lasts for several weeks. The pollen and nectar soon attract beetles, but during the day more useful visitors arrive to feed. They include sunbirds—Africa's closest equivalent to hummingbirds—and also the Cape sugarbird, which lives only where proteas bloom. As these birds probe the flower heads with their slender beaks, their foreheads become covered with pollen, and they transfer this to the next flower head they visit. During the Cape sugarbird's breeding season, it can visit up to 250 flower heads a day. The bird not only gets its food from the protea flower, it also uses parts of the flower to build its nest. The protea's fluffy seeds, in particular, make a cosy nest lining.

There are more than a hundred kinds of proteas, and at least half of them use birds to spread their pollen. Thousands of miles to the east, in Australia, shrubs called banksias have similar flower heads, and live in much the same way. Birds pollinate most banksias, but in western Australia a tiny marsupial called the honey possum pollinates some types. The honey possum feeds at night, and hides in old birds' nests during the day.

Spreading Seeds

In shrubland on a sunny day, listen for a distinctive sound. It's a sudden snap, followed by a brief pattering on the ground. This is the noise of exploding pods—just one of the ways that shrubs scatter their seeds.

Like most plants, shrubs scatter their seeds to give them the best chance of finding the space to grow. Exploding pods are grown by many pea-family shrubs. The pods work by building up tension, like someone winding up a spring. As sunshine dries the pod, the two sides try to twist. When the pod eventually splits open, the sides suddenly curl, flicking the seeds into the air.

A big pod can catapult seeds several yards away, safely out of the shade of the parent plant. But many shrubs scatter their seeds much farther. For real long-distance travel, they rely on one of two different methods: animals and the wind.

In return for a meal, birds do the seed-scattering work for figs and for other shrubs with juicy fruit. They eat the fruit and digest its succulent flesh but scatter the seeds unharmed in their droppings. If you ever wondered why shrubs often grow near

abandoned buildings and rocky outcrops, it's because this is where birds like to perch after they have eaten. Other shrubs take a more direct approach—they use hooks to fasten their seeds to animals' fur or feathers. Some of their hooks are too small to see, but a few—such as the African devil's claw—are as big as fingers, with sharply pointed tips. These hooks latch onto large mammals, allowing the seeds to hitch a lift for miles.

Many shrubs have feathery seeds that are easily blown by the breeze, but a few have their own unusual ways of using the wind. One of these plants is bladder senna, which grows pods that look like miniature balloons. When the pods are ripe, the wind breaks them off, and they bounce like small pieces of litter across the ground.

Primed by Fire

Seeds are usually scattered as soon as they are ripe, but some shrubs seem reluctant to let them go. Proteas and banksias shut theirs up inside old flower heads or tough pods. They can hold onto their seeds for more than twenty years. It seems like a strange thing to do, so why do they wait so long?

For these plants, fire is the key. They protect their seeds until there is a blaze, which clears away most of the plant matter on the ground. Once the flower heads or pods have been scorched, they open, dropping their seeds on a fertile bed of ash.

In California, greasewood has its own way of making sure that its seeds sprout at the right time. It drops its seeds soon after it flowers, but most of them then lie waiting in the soil. To sprout, they need to be heated to 1,200°F (650°C)—something that only happens when a blaze passes overhead.

However, it hedges its bets, because greasewood also produces seeds that don't need fire at all. These are triggered to sprout in the usual way—by getting wet.

Nature's Planters

Some plants have their seeds spread by ants carrying them away. This happens to the seeds of a type of protea called a common pagoda or *rooistompie* (left). The *rooistompie* lives in the fynbos of South Africa's Western Cape. Its seeds are coated with a substance attractive to ants, but the inner part of each seed is hard and difficult for ants to break open. When ants find these seeds, they quickly carry them underground. Once the ants have chewed off the tasty part, they leave the rest of the seed to germinate and grow into a new *rooistompie* plant.

The Mediterranean

The Mediterranean Sea is surrounded by rocky hillsides and studded with islands. Over several millennia, people have transformed the region, creating the shrublands that exist today.

In spring, tough shrubs such as spiny broom add a splash of color to the dry garigue shrubland on the coast of Corsica. In the undergrowth live shrews, hedgehogs, and lizards, while Sardinian warblers flit from bush to bush.

Fact File

▲ Much of the coast is made of limestone. It is worn down by the sea into craggy cliffs and islands.

▲ More than 100 million tourists visit the Mediterranean region every year, contributing to the greatest concentration of tourism on Earth.

▲ The Mediterranean climate is warmer and drier in the east. Here, summer temperatures can reach more than 100°F (38°C).

1. Algarve
This stretch of coast is popular with tourists but remains an important habitat for cork oaks and migrating birds.

2. Tell Plateau
In the days of the ancient Roman Empire, there were lions, cheetahs, and elephants here. Now there are olive groves and sparse, dry forests.

3. Balearic Islands
These tourist spots are a mixture of wild coasts covered with shrubland and beaches lined with high-rise hotels.

4. Provence
A region of France famous for its fields of lavender and for its food, flavored with local aromatic shrubs such as thyme.

5. Al Feidja National Park
A vital habitat for the endangered barbary deer.

6. Sicily
Sites such as the Zingaro Nature Reserve preserve the shrubby habitat of this island.

7. Dinaric Alps
A mountain range covered in pine forest and scrubby evergreen Mediterranean trees. It includes the beautiful Plitvice Lakes World Heritage Site.

8. Samaria Gorge, Crete
In the rugged White Mountains of Crete is the longest gorge in Europe, a popular site with walkers.

9. Thera (Santorini)
A center of the ancient Minoan civilization, before a volcanic eruption almost destroyed the island 3,500 years ago.

10. Al Chouf Reserve
This reserve protects the habitat of the Lebanese cedar, the emblem of Lebanon.

The Hoopoe

With its fan-shaped crest and black-and-white wings, the hoopoe is one of the most eye-catching birds of Mediterranean shrublands. Many hoopoes spend the winter in Africa and migrate to southern Europe in the spring. They breed in shrubby woodland and olive groves, probing into the earth with their long curved beaks to feed on insects and their grubs. Hoopoes nest in holes, either in trees or in the ground, and are famous for their unhygienic habits. They never clear out their nests, and they have a strong smell that probably helps deter other animals from attacking them.

Shrubland Animals

Shrublands can be tough going for people, but for many animals they are perfect places to live and find food.

The Mediterranean shrubland in summer is buzzing with insects. Crickets, such as this Provence cricket, make chirping sounds with their wings to attract a mate.

If shrublands were restaurants, the menu would run to dozens of pages. The animals that feed here include lots of meat eaters, but the ones with the greatest impact on plants are vegetarians. They are vital to shrubland life, because they become the food that predators and scavengers eat.

The Cape sugarbird visits the pincushion protea blooms of the South African fynbos to drink their nectar. In doing so, the bird pollinates the flowers.

Chewing It Over

In shrublands, plant food is often easy to find, but it's difficult to digest. Most of the plants are so tough, or so full of oils, that a person couldn't digest them at all. But shrubland plant eaters manage to thrive because they have special equipment to tackle this sort of food.

The largest shrubland plant eaters are hoofed mammals, such as antelope and deer. They are ruminants, which means they have complicated digestive systems that can deal with leaves. Instead of one stomach, they have four. The biggest—called the rumen—is packed with millions of microorganisms bathed in saliva (spit). The microorganisms are at home in these surroundings, and they earn their keep by releasing chemicals that break down chewed-up leaves. In return for doing this work, they get a small share of the food, and their host gets the rest.

Ruminants need tough teeth to tear off and chew up their food, particularly if they feed on shrubs. To make sure that their microorganisms can do a thorough job, they

bring up the food they have swallowed, and chew it a second time. This is called ruminating, or chewing the cud. Cattle are ruminants, and they often chew the cud lying down. But antelope and deer live in a more dangerous environment. They chew the cud while standing up, so that they can be ready to make a quick escape.

Antelope and Deer

If you imagine a herd of antelope, the chances are that you will think of them on Africa's grassy plains. But not all antelope live in grassland, and not all of them come from Africa. Many species spend some of their time in shrubland, and some of them never stray onto grassland at all. In shrubland, there is more cover from prying eyes. There are also more places where females can conceal their newborn calves.

Grassland antelope live in large herds for safety. In shrubland, where it is easier to hide from predators, antelope often live in family groups rather than big herds. Many antelope are small, since shrubland can be difficult to move through. One of the smallest is Kirk's dik dik, a miniature antelope from eastern Africa. It can weigh as little as 6 pounds (3 kg), and its slender shape allows it to dash through the densest thickets. When it runs off, it makes a sharp "dik dik" cry, warning its relatives that danger is nearby.

Most shrubland antelope live in the tropics. Deer, on the other hand, generally live in cooler parts of the world. They can look very similar to antelope, but they are easy to tell apart: Male deer grow antlers, while antelope of both sexes have horns.

The gerenuk is an antelope that browses thorny shrubs in Ethiopia, Somalia, and northern Kenya. Standing on its hind legs for long periods, it takes only the most nutritious morsels it can find.

Bee-eaters are colorful and conspicuous birds of the Mediterranean shrubland. During courtship, a male bee-eater offers a gift of food to his intended mate.

Antelope's horns are made of keratin, the same material that forms hair and fingernails. Deer's antlers, however, are made of bone, and they fall off and regrow each year. For deer, growing antlers is a demanding business—there is often more bone in a single antler than in a whole human arm.

More than a dozen kinds of deer live in shrublands, and the North American mule deer is one of the biggest. Its antlers have lots of prongs and can measure 4 feet (1.2 m) from tip to tip. Despite its size, the mule deer moves quietly and seldom gives itself away. It needs to be secretive because its chief predator—the mountain lion—is efficient and deadly. An adult mountain lion can eat a fully grown mule deer every two weeks, but during the breeding season, a female with cubs might kill a deer every three days.

Despite this danger, mule deer are very successful animals, thanks partly to their flexible diet. They eat hundreds of different

 ## Famous Flies

In Australia's bush, summer brings an unwelcome insect—the bushfly. This small fly doesn't bite, but it does have a strong liking for the moisture and salt on human skin. To satisfy its craving, it settles on people's faces and even crawls into their nostrils and their ears. Bushflies start life as maggots in animal droppings before transforming into adult flies in the soil. When the fly season is at its height, clouds of them fill the air. The only way to keep them off is to wear a hat with a net, or a hat with corks on strings.

Mallee Animals

The mallee shrublands in Australia have a unique mixture of animals. Many of them rely on the shrublands and can't live in the surrounding desert. Bandicoots, for example, are small marsupials that use the dense cover of mallee shrubland to hide from predators, while ant-eating marsupials called numbats forage in dead wood for ants and termites. Certain legless lizards and snakes also rely on the dead wood and leaf litter that build up in mallee shrublands. They use the dead plant material as both hiding place and hunting ground.

Unfortunately for shrubland animals, the climate is ideal for farming, and much of the land has been cleared. The western swamp tortoise has suffered more than most. Not only has it lost habitat, but it is hunted by cats and foxes, and killed by frequent bushfires triggered by people. Only 300 tortoises survive. They live in a patch of habitat near Perth.

plants, and they feed on twigs and bark when leaves are hard to find. It's the ultimate in high-fiber food, but with their on-board microorganisms, deer can break it down.

The Night Watch

Compared to deer, the small plant-eaters in shrublands can be very picky eaters. For example, the caterpillars of the two-tailed pasha butterfly feed only on the leaves of the strawberry tree, which grows around the Mediterranean Sea. Despite its tasty-sounding name, this small tree has flavorless fruit, and its leaves taste even worse. Most animals avoid them, but pasha caterpillars eat nothing else. By concentrating on this undesirable food, they almost have it to themselves. For birds, though, the warty red fruit are a valuable source of food in winter.

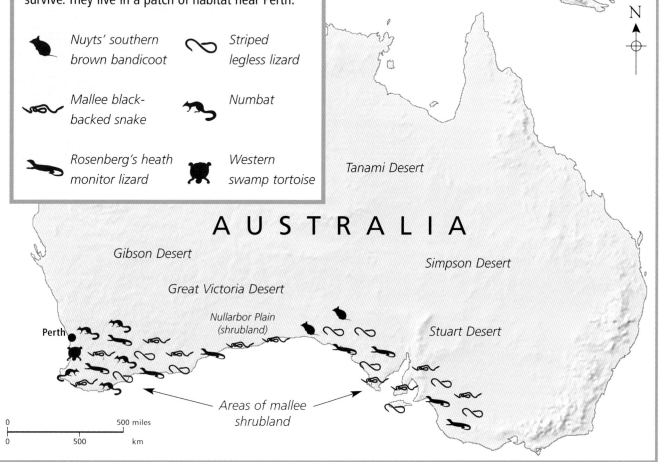

Nuyts' southern brown bandicoot		Striped legless lizard	
Mallee black-backed snake		Numbat	
Rosenberg's heath monitor lizard		Western swamp tortoise	

N

Tanami Desert

AUSTRALIA

Gibson Desert

Simpson Desert

Great Victoria Desert

Nullarbor Plain (shrubland)

Stuart Desert

Perth

Areas of mallee shrubland

| 0 | | 500 miles |
| 0 | 500 | km |

In North America, several kinds of grasshoppers feed entirely on the creosote bush, an ultra-tough desert shrub. The caterpillars benefit in the same way: Hardly anything else is interested in the bush's oily leaves, so the caterpillars don't compete with any other animals for food.

Grasshoppers are good at jumping away from danger, so they can risk feeding during the day. But in shrublands, most plant-eating insects avoid the daylight and feed under the cover of darkness. As dusk falls and grasshoppers stop chirping, crickets and katydids begin their noisy chorus, signaling the start of the night shift.

These animals are relatives of grasshoppers, and they have a similar shape, with a long body, tough jaws, and strong legs. They also call in a similar way, by scraping parts of their bodies together. Many are amazingly well camouflaged—even with a bright flashlight they are difficult to find. But if you do track one down, don't be surprised if you find it munching a fellow insect, instead of leaves or flowers. Crickets and katydids are not strict

Turning Up the Heat

Mallee fowls of Australia have a bizarre way of keeping their eggs warm. Instead of sitting on them, these shrubland birds build giant compost heaps from fallen leaves and lay their eggs inside. When the leaves start to rot they give off heat, and this makes the eggs develop. The heap has to be at just the right temperature, and the parents check it by using their beaks like thermometers. If it is too hot, they scrape away some of the leaves, but if it is too cool, they pile more on. Once the eggs hatch, the chicks struggle to the surface. Their parents do not feed them, so they wander off to start life on their own.

vegetarians, and many have a soft spot for animal food. If an insect lands nearby, it risks being grabbed and eaten.

Insect Eaters

With so many insects on the move, shrublands are ideal hunting grounds for insect eaters. These hunters include birds, lizards, spiders, and centipedes, as well as insects themselves. Crickets and katydids are only part-time hunters, but many other insects—such as assassin bugs and praying mantises—never touch plant food.

These useful but alarming animals have different ways of dealing with their prey. An assassin bug stabs its prey, then sucks up the victim's juices through a syringe-like mouth.

The ocellated lizard is one of the largest and most handsome of the Mediterranean's many lizards. A true Mediterranean species, it lives as far north as the most northerly olive trees but no farther.

Once an assassin has drained the victim dry, it usually drops the remains of its meal. A young assassin bug, however, sometimes stacks the dried-out bodies on its back—camouflage of a gruesome and unusual kind that disguises it from its prey. Praying mantises are much more thorough: They eat the whole corpse. A mantis usually starts with the head, then slowly works toward the tail, cutting up the crunchy outer skeleton with its efficient jaws.

Lizards hunt insects in most of the world's shrublands, usually on the ground. But in Africa and southern Asia, some lizards stalk their prey in shrubs and trees. These are chameleons—peculiar animals that are famous for being able to change color.

 ## Spiked by a Shrike

Shrublands are the favorite habitat of shrikes—starling-sized songbirds that behave like miniature birds of prey. They hunt grasshoppers, mice, and even other birds, and they have a grisly habit of spiking their dead victims by pushing them onto thorns. Shrikes do not have the powerful talons of large birds of prey, so they need to spike their prey to make it easier to tear apart. Each shrike (right) has a larder in a favorite tree or shrub, where it keeps a collection of impaled corpses. Their larders are useful stores for times when food is scarce.

Instead of running like most lizards do, chameleons creep stealthily along branches, gripping them with their toes and their tails. Their eyes can swivel independently, so they can see in two different directions at once. When a chameleon spots an insect, it slows down until it is moving no faster than a snail. As soon as the insect is in range, the chameleon shoots out its tongue and instantly hauls in its catch. A chameleon's tongue can be as long as the rest of its body, and the tongue has a sticky tip that makes sure there is no escape for the insect.

Chameleons are well camouflaged, but in shrublands some of the best disguises belong to birds. In Europe, the common nightjar spends the daytime resting on the ground, where its mottled brown feathers make it look exactly like a piece of a fallen

Below: Praying mantises stalk the shrublands of South Africa, hunting by stealth and ambush. They catch prey by rapidly extending their long, folded front legs and stabbing their victim with spines on the inner surface.

Left: Most of chameleons' color changes are not for camouflage. Instead, they usually change color to communicate with other chameleons.

Shrubland Rodents

Compared to leaves, seeds are packed with energy. They are also easier to digest, and much easier to store. This explains why there are lots of seed eaters in shrublands, even though seeds can sometimes be tricky to find.

Rodents are the real experts at this lifestyle because they are well equipped for carrying their food back home. Their secret is a pair of built-in cheek pouches, which can fill up like stretching shopping bags. The pouches can be closed off from the rest of the mouth, so a rodent can eat or drink even when its pouches are full. For their size, hamsters and

Right: A tawny frogmouth's huge mouth funnels flying insects into its stomach during nighttime hunting. During the day, it can put on a frightening display.

branch. But when the sun sets, the branch miraculously comes to life and takes off. The nightjar has a short beak but a very wide mouth, fringed with feathery bristles. It is a living funnel that catches moths and other insects on the wing after dark.

In the Australian bush, another of these nocturnal birds, the tawny frogmouth, pounces on its prey from a perch. During the day, it sits bolt upright with its eyes almost closed, making itself look like a piece of dead wood. But if anything comes too close, it suddenly opens its cavernous mouth, revealing bright pink skin inside. With luck, this display frightens the intruder away, otherwise the frogmouth would have to escape or end up as a meal itself.

The California pocket mouse forages at night under the shrub canopy. When it's cheek pouches are full of seeds, it stores more seeds in underground chambers. Those that it forgets may sprout into new shrubs.

American pocket mice have some of the largest pouches of all. Theirs reach back as far as their shoulders, so they can carry hundreds of small seeds at a time.

Shrubland rodents range from the dormice and spiny mice of the Mediterranean to the giant tuco-tuco and the lesser mara (which looks like a small deer) in the Gran Chaco of South America. Many are good climbers, but most prefer to collect seeds that have fallen to the ground. Their main harvest is usually in the summer, but with some careful searching, they can turn up seeds at other times. In the chaparral of California, pocket mice do this by sifting the soil with their front paws. These have long front claws, which help sort seeds from the soil. Once a pocket mouse has collected a pawful, it transfers the seeds to its cheek pouches, ready for the journey back to base.

Seed-Eating Birds

For safety, rodents do their seed collecting at night, when there is less chance of being attacked. Seed-eating birds cannot see well after dark, so they collect their food by day. To avoid getting eaten, both rodents and birds have to stay on the lookout and be ready to run or fly away.

Tinamous, which live in South American scrub, take off only as a last resort. If danger threatens, these chicken-sized birds run for cover, before suddenly freezing, which makes them hard to see. But if something is hot on their trail, they take emergency action and burst into the air on stubby wings. Being exposed in the air is risky, and they don't fly far. Once they have dropped back into the scrub, they seem to disappear instantly.

 # Worm Lizards

Underneath the dry scrub of northwest Mexico, one of the world's strangest animals hunts its prey. It's the ajolote—a pink, wormlike reptile with just one pair of legs. Its legs are small and stubby and are positioned just behind its head. The ajolote thrusts its head forward through the soil to create its burrow, and feeds on the termites and worms it finds as it moves along. It belongs to a group of reptiles called amphisbaenians, or worm lizards. Worm lizards live on most continents, but people rarely see them and we don't know much about their lives.

Throughout the world's shrublands, many seed-eating birds behave in a similar way. By sticking to the ground until the last possible minute, they make themselves harder to find. But the biggest seed eaters cannot fly at all, because their wings are far too small. These flightless giants include the rhea of South America and the emu of Australia. Emus can form roving flocks hundreds strong. The ostrich of Africa also wanders into shrubland, although it is more at home on grassy plains.

For a land bird, not being able to fly might sound disastrous, but all of these seed-eating species manage. The chief reason for this is that they have extremely good eyesight and marathon-runners' legs. With their long necks, they can peer above the vegetation around them, and within seconds they can be speeding away. They can run for 20 or 30 minutes at a time, which is enough to give most of their enemies the slip.

Seed-eating birds don't only swallow seeds; many also gulp down insects and the occasional stone. Stones lodge in a muscular chamber called the crop, which is in front of a bird's stomach. Here the stones help in grinding up food so it is easier to digest. Birds are not very good at telling stones from other hard objects that they find lying around. This explains why ostriches swallow coins and bottle caps, or even car keys if they get the chance.

Snake Alert

If you're planning a walk in shrubland, it's worth remembering that it's an ideal habitat for snakes. Shrubs themselves can hide plenty of prey, while the spaces between

them are tailor-made for basking in the sun. Most snakes are harmless to people, but even so, wear thick, ankle-high boots and watch where you put your feet—and your hands.

Most shrubland snakes slither away the moment they sense approaching human feet. They can hear you approach by detecting vibrations traveling through the soil. But in tropical shrubland, some snakes have trouble doing this because they spend their lives off the ground. One of the most remarkable of these climbers is the brown vine snake, which is distributed all the way from the southwestern United States to Brazil. It grows up to 5 feet (1.5 m) long, and its slender body and pointed snout make it look just like the stem of a climbing plant. The disguise tricks lizards, which are the vine snake's favorite

Rheas' diets are varied in the South American chaco, and when they get the chance, rheas eat almost any crop grown by people. So they are hunted, and many end up as leather products or even dog food.

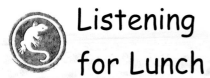 Listening
for Lunch

Africa's shrubland and grassland is home to the bat-eared fox—a dainty mammal that uses giant ears to listen for its food. It feeds after dark on beetles and termites, and it tracks them down almost entirely by sound. Its teeth are much smaller than those of other foxes, and it has eight extra ones at the back of its jaws to help it squash and chew its food.

Like the vine snakes of the North and South American shrublands, Africa's twig snakes hide by pretending to be twigs or stems.

prey, and it often fools people as well. To make its camouflage even more effective, the snake spends most of the time keeping absolutely still. If someone comes too close, it tries the same trick as the tawny frogmouth, and opens its mouth wide in the hope of frightening the intruder away.

Although the brown vine snake is poisonous, its bite does people little harm. The same isn't true of the most feared of North American snakes—the rattlesnakes. The red diamond rattlesnake is a chaparral specialist and, like all vipers, has long hinged fangs that inject venom into prey. It is a species in decline, though, and does not need persecuting by people.

The snakes in Australia's shrublands have particularly potent venom, but as far as people are concerned, the most dangerous of all shrubland snakes is probably the black mamba. This African species is an amazingly rapid climber, and even quicker on the ground. It grows to 15 feet (3 m) long and can move at 12 mph (20 km/h), so it can outrun a child. Small mammals and birds make up most of its prey, but its venom can easily kill people, too.

Top Predators

Most animals have some natural enemies, but a few are so large and powerful that they have none once they are fully grown. These are the biome's top predators—hunters that have nothing to fear apart from people and the changes that people cause. The mountain lion, or puma, is a top predator in California's chaparral, while the leopard is top predator in most of the shrublands of Africa. Big cats are now very rare around the Mediterranean, so the top predators there

are eagles and other large birds of prey. In Australia and a few islands in Indonesia, the top shrubland predators are not big cats, birds, or even snakes but giant lizards.

These lizards belong to a family called the monitors, which contains about 45 species. In Australia, the largest shrubland variety is the lace monitor, which grows up to 6 feet (2 m) long. Its powerful legs make it a good climber, and it has sharp claws that it uses to rip apart prey. But even this animal is dwarfed by the largest monitor of all: the Komodo dragon, which lives in forest and scrub in Indonesia. The heaviest specimens can weigh twice as much as an adult person, and measure 10 feet (3 m) from head to tail.

Komodo dragons feed on almost anything they can find, from live deer and snakes to dead remains. They have a keen sense of smell and can track down carcasses from up to 3 miles (5 km) away. Once fully grown, they can expect to live for up to forty years, but not all of them get a chance. Adult Komodo dragons often behave as cannibals, and young ones can end up as a meal.

A Komodo dragon can kill with just one bite. Bacteria in the lizard's saliva infect the victim's wound, crippling it. Sooner or later, the lizard tracks down its hobbling quarry by smell.

43

The Fynbos

South Africa's Cape region is small, but its shrubland—the fynbos—contains almost as many types of flowering plants as the whole of Europe.

Proteas, with their distinctive, leathery leaves, and ericas, with their clusters of small flowers, are both common in the fynbos shrublands.

Fact File

▲ The Cape region covers less than a thousandth of the world's land surface but is home to more than 8,000 species of plants.

▲ 70 percent of fynbos plants live nowhere else.

▲ More than eight hundred species of heathers live in southern Africa, mainly in the fynbos.

▲ Because of the richness and distinctiveness of the fynbos plants, scientists classify the Cape region, despite its small size, as one of the world's six floral kingdoms.

Kalahari Desert

Namib Desert

NAMIBIA

Orange River

SOUTH

Veld

AFRICA

9

4 K a r o o

AFRICA

Namaqualand

Vanrhynsdorp •

Atlantic

Skilpad
Wildflower
Reserve

G r e a t   E s c a r p m e n t

5

7 Mountain Zebra
National Park

Ocean

3

N

8 Addo Elephant
National Park

G r e a t   K a r o o

Wilderness
National Park

Cape Town •

Little Karoo

Table
Mountain **1**

Tsitsikamma
National Park

Port Elizabeth •

Cape Peninsula
National Park **2**

George •

Humansdorp

Cape of
Good Hope

6

0   300 miles

0   300   km

---

1. Table Mountain
This famous flat-topped mountain dominates Cape Town, which lies below.

2. Cape Peninsula National Park
Rugged coastline and richly varied fynbos plant life attract visitors to this park.

3. Skilpad Wildflower Reserve
A reserve named for the Afrikaans word for the tortoises that come to drink here. Visitors come to see the spring display of flowers such as Namaqualand daisies.

4. Karoo
The Karoo region is drier than the fynbos, and the plant life is succulent (fleshy).

5. Great Escarpment
A ridge that separates the high plateaus of the interior from the coastal plains.

6. Tsitsikamma National Park
This strip of rocky coastline has deep river gorges, fynbos plants, and forests of giant yellowwood. Visitors can see deer, antelope, baboons, and vervet monkeys.

7. Mountain Zebra National Park
This park protects the shrubland habitat of a critically endangered subspecies (local type) of zebra, the Cape mountain zebra.

8. Addo Elephant National Park
Spiny and succulent shrubs form dense thickets here. Tourists can watch wildlife at night beside a floodlit water hole.

9. Veld
A type of grassland that covers much of South Africa's interior.

 # Fynbos Zebras

Fynbos plants are tough and unappetizing, and few large mammals live off them. One exception is the Cape mountain zebra. At one time, thousands of these zebras roamed the fynbos but were easy to hunt, and by the 1930s fewer than fifty were left. Since then, a conservation program has helped the zebra survive. More than two hundred live at the Mountain Zebra National Park, and several hundred are at large in other parts of the fynbos. The Cape mountain zebra has been luckier than its close relative, the quagga. This animal, a kind of zebra whose stripes faded to brown toward its rear, lived in open, dry country but was hunted to extinction by 1883.

45

People and Shrublands

The shrubland landscape, often full of dry, impenetrable, thorny plant life, can look unwelcoming. But the land yields food for hunters, gatherers, goatherds, and farmers.

Shrublands might not look like the ideal place to set up home, particularly if you are used to city streets. But shrublands have a lot of the things people need. In many kinds of shrubland, there is a year-round supply of food—as long as you know where to collect it or how to catch it.

People who live entirely on wild food are termed hunter-gatherers. Theirs is humanity's oldest lifestyle, requiring little equipment but a lot of experience and skill. Being a hunter-gatherer isn't easy. Today, very few people live by hunting and gathering, but there are a few places where this difficult way of life is still practiced.

Hunter-Gatherers of the Chaparral
When Europeans first landed in California, in the mid 1500s, hunter-gatherers were the only people that lived in the chaparral. They

Aboriginal people have coped with huge changes since European settlers arrived in Australia. Some people still hunt for food in the shrublands, though.

did not grow crops or raise animals, but it was unusual for them to run short of food. They hunted deer, quail, and other animals, and collected fruit and seeds. Among the most important seeds were the acorns from prickly scrub oaks, which they ground up and used as flour. There may have been about 150,000 people in California as a whole, compared with more than 30 million today.

California's inhabitants had followed the hunting and gathering way of life for several thousand years. But as Spanish missionaries made their way northward from Mexico in the 1770s, things changed. The European arrivals established farms around their missions, which gave southern California's hunter-gatherers their first taste of a settled way of life. Farming was not the only thing the missionaries introduced. With them came a collection of European diseases, such as measles. For native Californians these infections often proved deadly, and the population started to fall.

Despite these changes, and the steadily growing number of Europeans, some of the chaparral's hunter-gatherers kept up their old way of life. However, in 1848, an event occurred that changed California forever. Gold was discovered in central California, and within a year, thousands of prospectors arrived over the mountains from the east as well as by ship after the dangerous passage around the southern tip of South America. With the miners came a host of traders and other arrivals, all eager to make a living. The Gold Rush was short lived, but the changes it brought were not. By 1900, towns, roads, and farms were spreading all over California, and most hunter-gatherers had disappeared.

The panic of the Gold Rush has long since died away, and shacks stand empty in the dry shrubland of Nevada and California.

Emu Wars

When Western Australia's shrublands were cleared to make way for wheat, the region's emus soon discovered that wheat was a major new supply of food. Thousands of these giant birds strode through the fields eating the crops. In 1932, things were so bad that the army was called in. A machine-gun unit was sent to bring the feathered marauders under control. The mission didn't go according to plan. The emu flocks split when they saw the soldiers approach, and most of the emus escaped unharmed. With the failure of the emu war, planners came up with a better solution: giant fences that keep the emus out of the wheat fields.

By today's standards, California's original inhabitants were very environmentally friendly. They used few raw materials and left behind almost no waste. They probably altered animal life by hunting, and it's likely that they affected plant life, as well, by starting fires. However, these changes would have been tiny compared to the changes caused by people today.

Australia's Aboriginal People

Experts believe that people arrived in California's shrublands at least 10,000 years ago, almost certainly from northeast Asia. But on the other side of the Pacific, in Australia, aboriginal people have lived in shrubland for at least four times as long. Like California's hunter-gatherers, aboriginal people lived entirely on wild food, and they followed a largely nomadic existence, sometimes moving hundreds of miles a year.

Today, many aboriginal people live in towns and cities, but in the outback, or "bush," some keep their hunter-gatherer skills alive. Here, the menu includes lots of edible plants, as well as marsupial mammals, birds,

and lizards. There are also Australian specialities such as water-holding frogs, which are a handy source of water during droughts. Early aboriginal people were experts in self-sufficiency, and they developed ways of getting the most food from the land. During dry weather, they set fire to dead plant matter, encouraging fresh green growth. The new growth attracted birds and other animals, which made hunting more successful.

Over many generations, this burning had some important effects on Australia's plant life. Types of trees and shrubs that are harmed by fire were slowly whittled away, leaving more space for species like mallees, which can resprout from their trunks or roots. Across huge areas of bush, fires started deliberately helped create the patchwork of shrubland and grassland that exists today.

Herding Animals

Australia's aboriginal people never raised animals for food, perhaps because the species that might have been useful—such as kangaroos—are difficult to control. But in the Mediterranean region, shrubland people had more suitable animals on their doorstep. The most valuable were sheep and goats, which have a handy instinct for sticking together in herds, instead of scattering when danger threatens. People gradually learned how to manage these herds and so obtain a permanent supply of meat and milk, and wool for making clothes.

Guarded by shepherds, sheep wandered across the landscape, nibbling plants with their extra-tough teeth. As the animals multiplied, so did their effects on the plant life. All the juiciest plants and saplings were trimmed to the ground, leaving only the plants that were tough, spiny, or too bad-tasting to eat. The Mediterranean shrubland slowly changed and also spread to occupy land formerly covered by trees.

Sure-Footed Browsers

Goats are amazingly nimble. They can clamber along sloping branches to get at leafy twigs, so very little is beyond their reach. In Morocco, goats forage for fruit in the argan tree (below). People obtain a cooking oil, prized for its flavor, by squeezing the hard nut of the argan fruit. According to folklore, only nuts chewed and spat out by the goats are used, but people also use simpler methods of harvesting the nuts!

The Greek island of Crete provides another example of where goats' climbing skills can lead. Generations of goats have stripped the hillsides, reducing much of the original forest to rock dotted with spiny shrubs. In places, the soil is washed away, making it harder for the plant cover to return.

The Start of Farming

In Europe and southwest Asia, people started herding sheep and goats about 10,000 years ago. But this way of life is not the only one that has changed the shrubland landscape. In that part of the world, people also collected plant food, including edible seeds from wild grasses. In southwest Asia, people discovered that it was better to grow these grasses themselves, so they could harvest the seeds more efficiently. This was the beginning of cereal farming—a way of life that has had a tremendous effect on shrublands, and also on many other biomes across the world.

Today, wild ancestors of wheat still grow around the Mediterranean and southwest Asia. When fully grown, these grasses are no more than knee-high, and it would take a lot of picking to collect enough grain for a loaf of bread. But from this unpromising start, early farmers selected the plants that produced the best yields, and used their

Artificial Shrublands

During the Stone Age of northwest Europe, people created a kind of shrubland called heath. Heath, or heathland, is an open landscape that was originally covered with forest. Early farmers cleared patches of forest to grow food. Heathland soil, however, is poor and sandy, so after a few years, the farmers often abandoned their clearings and moved on.

Once the farmers had gone, the trees were slow to return. Instead, the ground often became covered with heather and gorse—two shrubs that are good at surviving in poor soil. They created an ideal habitat for lizards, birds, and insects, including many species that could not live in the forest. These heathland inhabitants include some of northern Europe's largest grasshoppers and dragonflies, as well as many insect-eating birds.

seeds to plant their crops. After thousands of harvests, this process created the kind of wheat we grow today.

Corn also started life as a shrubland plant. Its wild ancestor is a grass called teosinte, which grows on rocky hillsides in Mexico. Teosinte looks unlike corn and has hundreds of tiny cobs, each with only a dozen seeds. People started growing teosinte about 7,000 years ago. Over time, the cobs of the farmed teosinte became fewer but much larger, and they also developed wraparound husks.

Corn is now the third most important cereal in the world, after wheat and rice. However, corn's husks prevent its seeds from scattering, so if people stopped planting corn, it would soon die out.

The ancestors of orange trees lived in tropical Asia, but cultivated ones are suited to the Mediterranean climate. Most grow in shrubland regions: Australia, South Africa, the Mediterranean, and California.

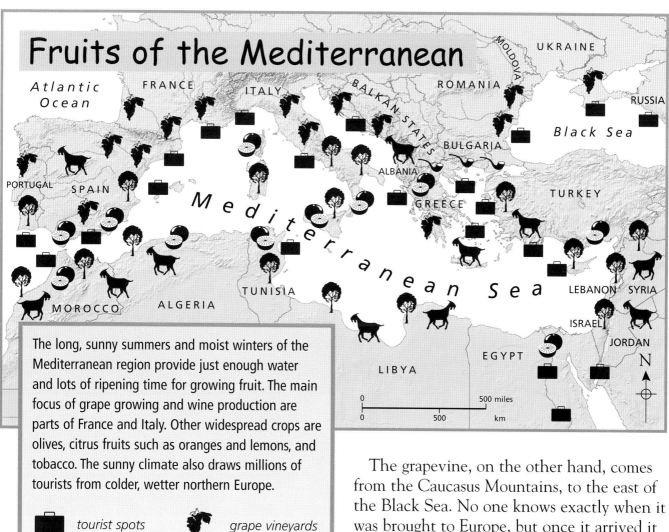

Fruits of the Mediterranean

The long, sunny summers and moist winters of the Mediterranean region provide just enough water and lots of ripening time for growing fruit. The main focus of grape growing and wine production are parts of France and Italy. Other widespread crops are olives, citrus fruits such as oranges and lemons, and tobacco. The sunny climate also draws millions of tourists from colder, wetter northern Europe.

tourist spots		grape vineyards	
tobacco farms		citrus orchards	
olive groves		goat grazing	

Shrubs That Yield Food

Cereals are not the only useful plants that thrive in shrubland regions. Where the summers are warm, olives and grapes are also very much at home. The olive tree originally lived in the eastern Mediterranean region. In Roman times, its oil was used for lighting as well as in cooking because it burns with a smoky yellow flame. The Romans also used it as an ingredient in soap and medicines, and even as suntan lotion. Now people grow it in groves throughout the Mediterranean.

The grapevine, on the other hand, comes from the Caucasus Mountains, to the east of the Black Sea. No one knows exactly when it was brought to Europe, but once it arrived it soon became a feature of the landscape, as more and more farmers started to make wine. Where space was short, hillsides were often cleared of their shrubs and terraced, creating vineyards that look like flights of stairs.

Many crop plants, such as tomatoes and potatoes, were brought to Europe from the Americas, but the olive and the grapevine traveled in the other direction. Spanish colonists took these plants across the Atlantic in the 1500s, and in the 1700s they arrived in Australia as well. Olive trees settled into their new surroundings, but the grapevines had an unexpected setback.

The guilty party was a small sap-sucking bug called phylloxera, which feeds on the roots and leaves of vines. North America's native vines can cope with this pest because

Grapevines love south-facing slopes, where they can ripen in the maximum amount of sunshine. So although sloping land is difficult to farm, many vineyards, such as this one in Spain, are planted on steep slopes.

they have lived with it for a very long time. European grapevines cannot, and after a bad attack they often die. During the mid-1800s, the bug found its way to Europe, and the results were catastrophic. Within about twenty years, very many of the continent's vines were destroyed. Grape growers then found that the bug cannot attack European grapevines that have been grafted onto American roots. Almost all of today's grapevines are combination plants, with tops and bottoms from two different continents.

Wildlife in Retreat

For adaptable animals, such as crows and coyotes, farms in shrublands have brought the chance of extra food. There are easy pickings around farm buildings, and sometimes plenty to eat in fields. But for many other shrubland animals, particularly those with specialized diets, things have not turned out so well. Without natural plant cover to eat or hide in, such animals have declined or become extinct.

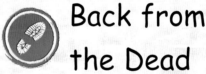 ## Back from the Dead

The clearing of shrub in the Australian southwest has placed some of the small marsupials that lived there in critical trouble. The mouse-sized dibbler (above) may be down to a few hundred individuals. It nests in fallen logs and needs dense shrubland to survive. For more than 80 years, everyone thought the dibbler was extinct, but it was rediscovered on the mainland in 1967, and then on Boullanger Island and Whitlock Island, off the west coast, in 1985. Perth Zoo is now breeding dibblers in captivity and establishing them in the wild nearby on tiny Escape Island.

Some of the most vulnerable shrubland species are those of southwest Australia. In the first half of the 20th century, bulldozers cleared away millions of acres of plants. The result was one of the most important wheat-growing regions in the world: good news for people, but bad news for the shrubland's unique native mammals.

Southwest Australia

Southwest Australia is like an island, cut off from the rest of the continent by deserts. Its flat, sandy soil is home to an incredible variety of shrubs and other plants, most of which grow nowhere else in the world.

In spring, parakeelya flowers carpet the ground in mulga shrubland, which blends into desert to the north and west. The mulga tree is a type of acacia.

Cape Range National Park

Great Sandy Desert

WESTERN

Mulga shrubland

4

Gibson Desert

AUSTRALIA

Shark Bay

Kalbarri National Park

2

Kalbarri

7

Kalgoorlie

Boullanger, Whitlock, and Escape Islands

Darling Range

Wheat belt

Perth

Mount Cook

6

Rottnest Island

1

Stirling Range

5

Jarrah-Karri Forest

Bluff Knoll

3

Fitzgerald River National Park

Walpole-Nornalup National Park

```
0                    200  miles
0        200          km
```

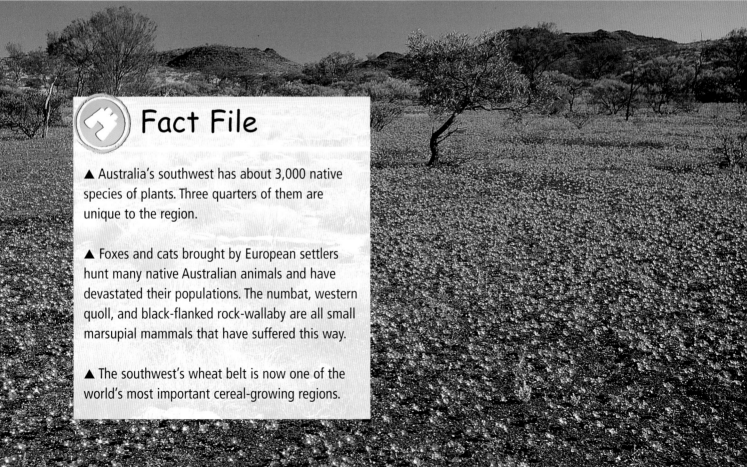

Fact File

▲ Australia's southwest has about 3,000 native species of plants. Three quarters of them are unique to the region.

▲ Foxes and cats brought by European settlers hunt many native Australian animals and have devastated their populations. The numbat, western quoll, and black-flanked rock-wallaby are all small marsupial mammals that have suffered this way.

▲ The southwest's wheat belt is now one of the world's most important cereal-growing regions.

AUSTRALIA

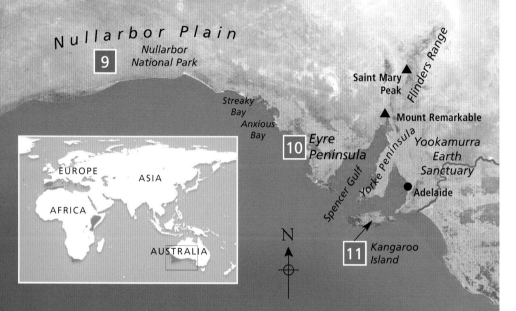

SOUTH
AUSTRALIA

8

Great
Victoria Desert

Nullarbor Plain

9

Nullarbor
National Park

Flinders Range

Saint Mary
Peak

Streaky
Bay

Anxious
Bay

Mount Remarkable

10

Eyre
Peninsula

Yorke Peninsula

Spencer Gulf

Yookamurra
Earth
Sanctuary

Adelaide

EUROPE

ASIA

AFRICA

AUSTRALIA

N

11

Kangaroo
Island

Spring Flowers

Southwest Australia's great natural flower show begins in August, which in this region is the beginning of spring. The blooms on display include many bizarre and colorful plants, from banksias and bottlebrushes to wax flowers and orchids. One of the most spectacular plants is the Australian Christmas tree, which is covered in intense yellow flowers from December to January. It belongs to the mistletoe family, but it is the only mistletoe in the world that grows into a tree. Western Australia's state flower is the red and green kangaroo paw (right).

It is covered in a bright red furry coat of hairs and looks a bit like the front paw of a kangaroo.

1. Rottnest Island
Originally a prison, this island is now a refuge for endangered animals such as the quokka, a kind of miniature kangaroo.

2. Kalbarri National Park
A park famous for its dramatic gorges and its spring display of wildflowers, such as banksias and the Kalbarri spider orchid.

3. Jarrah-Karri Forest
This moister region is covered by giant eucalyptus trees up to 300 feet (90 m) tall.

4. Mulga Shrubland
Emus stroll among the acacia trees in this dry shrubland, which is virtually semidesert.

5. Stirling Range
The dry shrublands in these mountains contain 1,500 species of plants, 87 of which grow nowhere else.

6. Wheat Belt
An area of cleared shrubland, the wheat belt is now the center of southwest Australia's cereal farming industry.

7. Kalgoorlie
A gold-mining town founded in the 1890s during southwestern Australia's Gold Rush.

8. Great Victoria Desert
The desert acts as a natural barrier to the movement of animals and plants between the southwest and other parts of Australia's shrubland.

9. Nullarbor Plain
Saltbushes cover this flat land for hundreds of miles.

10. Eyre Peninsula
Kangaroos and emus browse the gum trees and acacias in this region of mallee shrubland.

11. Kangaroo Island
There are no foxes or rabbits here, so native shrubland animals such as the rare heath monitor, a large lizard, flourish.

The Future

With pressure from people increasing all the time, the world's remaining shrublands face a fight for survival.

Compared to some biomes, shrublands don't often hit the headlines. Most of us know about "saving the rain forests," but "saving the shrublands" doesn't sound so urgent or appealing. But across the world, conservationists are trying to protect shrublands from a range of threats.

Heathland and Houses

In northwest Europe, pockets of heathland still survive from Stone Age times, when people first cleared trees to grow crops. Until a hundred years ago, these remnants from the past were kept clear of trees by ponies and sheep, and by people collecting firewood. With the arrival of modern farming,

heathland fell into disuse, and temperate forest reclaimed many patches. Today, the surviving heathland faces a new danger: the rapid spread of houses and roads.

Heathland is threatened all over northern Europe, but it is particularly at risk in southern England. In this busy part of the world, many people need homes, and patches of heathland often seem good places to build them. Altogether, more than three-quarters of England's heathland has disappeared.

If Stone Age farmers came back to Europe today, they would be amazed to see how the countryside has changed. But they might also be impressed by the efforts being made to preserve the heathlands that do remain.

Shrub Corridors

In Western Australia, farmers have cleared huge areas of natural shrubland. But along the state's main highways, strips of shrubland remain. These remnants have become important wildlife corridors, despite the danger from passing road traffic. The narrow wildlife corridors allow animals to travel from one area of shrubland to another. For marsupials like the long-nosed potoroo, these corridors are an essential lifeline. Without them, populations of potoroos would be cut off from each other. They would not be able to intermingle, and their numbers would soon fall.

Northwest Europe's heathland (main picture) is not natural. People and farm animals have been shaping it for centuries. But wildlife such as this dragonfly now rely on this human-created habitat for survival, so preserving heathland is a new target for conservationists.

Across Europe, from Denmark to Spain, a network of conservation organizations has been set up, and many threatened areas of heathland are now protected. This comes just in time for some of Europe's dragonflies, and also for birds like nightjars, because heathlands are among their most important breeding grounds.

Problem Plants

For wildlife, Europe's shrublands are important, but South Africa's fynbos is unique. Fynbos may not have towering trees or animals with star appeal, but its sheer variety makes it one of the botanical wonders of the world. It's a treasure that scientists are working hard to preserve.

Across much of the fynbos region, farming is the major threat, but there are other problems apart from cattle and goats. Over the last 150 years, people have introduced many different trees and shrubs into South Africa from various parts of the world. Some

of these introduced species now grow and spread wildly and threaten to swamp the fynbos's own plant life.

It's no surprise that the most successful of these plants come from Australia, because southwest Australia's climate and soil are very similar to South Africa's. The Australian invaders include small trees such as wattles, which have beautiful flowers but a tendency to spread. Wattles were originally planted for ornament, and for their bark, which can be used for tanning leather. They outgrew their usefulness long ago, however, and are now a serious pest. Some of them have infiltrated the coastal fynbos, while others have spread up mountains or over farmland. To protect the fynbos, conservationists have to remove these alien plants—a difficult task because they often resprout after they are cut down.

South Africa is not the only shrubland region where plant invaders have moved in. European plants, including many low-growing weeds, have escaped into California's chaparral. In turn, some African plants have also escaped in Australia, where they have proved just as good at causing problems.

One of the most successful of these African intruders is the scented

Giant tortoises can't compete for food with the herds of goats that people have brought to the Galápagos Islands. In future, goats must be excluded from areas so that some of the tortoises have enough to eat.

Back to Nature?

Santa Catalina Island, 26 miles (40 km) off the
California coast near Los Angeles, was once covered
by chaparral. But in the 1800s, people introduced
goats to the island. The goats tended to eat every
green morsel of the chaparral plants, and the habitat
started to disappear. Since then, the clock has been
turning back. People have hunted the goats to reduce
their numbers, and the last few hundred goats are
now being caught and released on the California
mainland. Conservationists hope that without attack
by goats, the natural chaparral plant life will recover.

thorn, which is a kind of acacia and related
to Australia's wattles. It is spreading fast,
creating a kind of shrubland that looks
more like Africa than Australia.

Introduced Animals

In some parts of the world, shrublands are
also threatened by animals that people bring
in from outside. The worst offenders are cats,
foxes, rats, and goats—species that harm
native animals and plants by eating them,
spreading disease, and by competing with
them for food. The troublesome newcomers
are a major problem on remote islands, where
they often have no natural enemies. In the
Galápagos Islands, for example, goats have

stripped much of the shrubland that covers
the dry volcanic soil. Faced with these
competitors, the islands' giant tortoises
have a much harder time finding food.

Around the world, conservationists are
trying to tackle the problems created by
introduced animals. On small islands, it is
sometimes possible to remove enough of the
invaders to bring the situation under control.
But on a landmass as gigantic as Australia,
trapping would never work. Conservation
workers here are trying an alternative that
relies on Australian plants. The plants in
question are poison peas, which grow mainly
in western Australia. These low-growing
shrubs contain a substance that is deadly to
most introduced mammals, such as foxes and
wild cats. Australia's marsupials, on the other
hand, are largely immune to the poison,
because they have adapted to local plants
over millions of years.

Island foxes of the California Channel Islands are not introduced pests but rare native animals that live nowhere else. Scientists are studying them to predict whether the foxes will avoid extinction.

Scientists have isolated the poison pea's poison and used it in baits. So far, the results are encouraging: In treated areas, the numbers of foxes and wild cats have fallen, and several species of endangered marsupials have started to make a comeback. One of the biggest poison-baiting programs is in Western Australia, where more than a dozen kinds of marsupial are on the brink of extinction.

With native mammals back in action, visiting flowers and spreading seeds, native shrubs also stand to gain from the eradication of foxes and wild cats. However, killing animals is a controversial business, even if it is done with conservation in mind. Many Australians, particularly city-dwelling cat owners, think it should stop, even though it seems to help native wildlife.

All Change?

Most shrublands exist in places where the climate is difficult for trees. A change in climate in the future might enable trees to grow on land now occupied by shrubland. Climate change could be one of the biggest problems for Earth's shrublands. The world's climate alters all the time, but scientists believe that it is now warming more quickly than it has done for thousands of years. Many scientists argue that people have triggered this change by polluting the atmosphere.

It is difficult to forecast the effects of rapid warming. However, according to most predictions, the tropics (regions of Earth near the equator) will become wetter. Africa's shrublands could become much more lush, and the long dry season might even become a thing of the past. If this happens, shrublands and savannas would be replaced by woodland, changing large swaths of the African landscape. In South America, similar changes would affect the shrublands of eastern Brazil. Here, drought is a common problem, so as far as people are concerned, it might be a welcome change.

By contrast, regions just outside the tropics, such as the Mediterranean and southern California, are likely to become drier. Summer droughts here are already long, and if they grow even longer, some shrubs will be tested to their limits. The toughest species, such as sagebrush, might persist, but those that need more moisture might not survive.

Adapting to the Future

Because Earth's climate is always changing, this is not the first time that shrubland plants and animals have had to adjust to new conditions. When conditions change, animals can move home quite easily, and so can plants, although they take longer because they spread by scattering seeds.

So how will the world's shrublands fare over the next hundred years? Shrublands will certainly be with us, although they might not stay in exactly the same places as they are today. Some shrubland plants and animals may lose out in the struggle to cope with climate change, and may disappear. Others may benefit from the changes and may blossom in their place.

But there will be other changes—changes involving us. Some experts predict that Earth's population will continue to increase dramatically until 2050 or 2070. After this, the population might remain steady or even fall. Then, at last, human pressure on shrublands will decrease. With luck, more of the world's shrublands will be protected, and people will appreciate the remarkable shrubland plants and animals even more than they do today.

 # Tourists to the Rescue

One way to preserve key areas of shrubland is to promote them as tourist attractions. The tourists' money pays for the management and protection of the preserved land. In South Africa, thousands of people visit the fynbos each year to see proteas and other plants growing wild. In Western Australia (below), the spectacular springtime wildflowers also attract lots of visitors. There are few roads, and much of the bush is inaccessible, so some companies offer helicopter rides to see these remote places. Farmers also grow some of the plants in wildflower farms, so people can pick the flowers without harming plants in the wild.

Glossary

aromatic: Having a strong smell.

atmosphere: The layer of air around Earth.

biome: A major division of the living world, distinguished by its climate and wildlife. Tundra, desert, and temperate grasslands are examples of biomes.

bug: A type of insect with sucking mouthparts, such as a phylloxera, an aphid, or an assassin bug.

camouflage: Natural disguise that makes animals or plants look like their surroundings.

cannibal: Animal that eats others of its own species.

canopy: A layer formed at the top of a forest by branches and leaves. Some shrublands have a broken canopy formed by shrubs.

carbon dioxide: A gas released when fuel burns. Carbon dioxide is one of the main gases thought to cause global warming.

chaco: A type of shrubland in South America, similar to chaparral. Also called matorral.

chaparral: Shrubland in southern California formed mainly by dense thickets of sages and evergreen oaks up to 8 feet (2.5 m) tall.

climate: The pattern of weather that happens in one place during an average year.

community: A collection of organisms living in the same place, such as a patch of woodland.

desert: A place that receives less than 10 inches (250 mm) of rain a year.

equator: An imaginary line around Earth, midway between the North and South poles.

eucalyptus: A type of plant native to Australia. Some eucalyptuses form mallee shrublands, others make up towering rain forests.

evaporate: To turn into gas. When water evaporates, it becomes water vapor, an invisible part of the air.

fynbos: Shrubland at the southern tip of South Africa formed mainly by proteas and heaths.

garigue: A sparse shrubland of the eastern Mediterranean region.

global warming: The gradual warming of Earth's climate, thought to be caused by pollution of the atmosphere.

greasewood: Also called chamise, this low, stiff shrub grows in the California chaparral.

heath: A general name for heathers and their relatives.

heath or heathland: An area covered by low shrubs such as heathers. Heath is usually an artificial habitat in Europe.

heather: A type of shrub with small leaves and bell-like flowers.

ice age: A period in history when Earth's climate was cooler and the polar ice caps expanded. The last ice age ended about 10,000 years ago.

lignotuber: A swollen, woody root storing food and water in some plants, such as mallees.

mallee: A small, shrubby, fire-resistant eucalyptus that grows in south and west Australia. Also, regions covered by mallee plants.

mammal: A warm-blooded animal that feeds its young on milk.

maquis: A type of shrubland that grows in the western Mediterranean region, formed by broad-leaved, evergreen shrubs.

marsupial: A type of mammal whose young develop in a pouch.

matorral: A type of shrubland in South America, similar to chaparral. Also called chaco.

microclimate: The pattern of weather within a small area, such as a valley, treetop, or burrow.

migration: A journey made by an animal to find a new home. Many animals migrate each year.

nectar: A sugary liquid produced by a plant to attract the animals that pollinate its flowers.

nomad: A person who travels from place to place in search of food and water, instead of settling permanently.

oxygen: A gas in the air. Animals and plants need to take in oxygen so their cells can release energy from food.

pollen: Dustlike particles produced by the male parts of a flower.

pollination: The transfer of pollen from the male part of a flower to the female part of the same flower or another flower, causing the flower to produce seeds.

predator: An animal that catches and eats other animals.

quail: A small, ground-living wild bird similar to a small chicken.

rain forest: A lush forest that receives frequent heavy rainfall.

ruminant: An animal with a complex digestive system of four stomachs. One stomach, the rumen, contains microorganisms that help digest tough plants.

sagebrush: A drought-resistant shrub with gray, aromatic leaves. It lives in the chaparral of North America and the Great Basin.

saltbush: A shrub that grows on the dry Nullarbor Plain, Australia.

scrub or scrubland: Alternative general names for shrubland.

shrubland: A biome that mainly contains shrubs, such as the chaparral of California.

species: A particular type of organism. Cheetahs are a species but birds are not, because there are lots of different bird species.

subtropics: A region of Earth within the temperate zone, but near, and similar to, the tropics.

temperate: Having a moderate climate. Earth's temperate zone lies between the warm, tropical regions and the cold, polar regions.

temperate forest: A biome that mainly contains tall broad-leaved trees. In Europe, it blends with shrubland in the south.

tropical: Within about 1,600 miles (2,575 km) of the equator. Tropical places are warm all year.

tropical forest: Forest in Earth's tropical zone, such as tropical rain forest or monsoon forest.

tropical grassland: A tropical biome in which grass is the main form of plant life.

tundra: A biome of the far north, made up of treeless plains covered with small plants.

venom: A poison injected by an animal using fangs or a sting.

wildlife corridor: A narrow strip of habitat that animals use for moving between larger patches of habitat.

Further Research

Books
Attenborough, David. *The First Eden: The Mediterranean World and Man.* Boston: Little, Brown, 1987.
Cowling, R., and Richardson, D. *Fynbos: South Africa's Unique Floral Kingdom.* Cape Town: Fernwood, 1995.
Dale, Nancy. *Flowering Plants: The Santa Monica Mountains, Coastal, and Chaparral Regions of Southern California.* Oakland: California National Park Service, 2000.
Ricciuti, Edward R. *Chaparral (Biomes of the World).* New York: Benchmark Books, 1996.

Websites
Wild World—Terrestrial Ecoregions of the World: www.nationalgeographic.com/wildworld/terrestrial.html
(A huge resource from National Geographic and the Worldwide Fund for Nature. Through a clickable map, you can access pictures and profiles of 867 ecoregions, which are like smaller divisions of biomes.)
Nature Base, Western Australia: www.calm.wa.gov.au/index.html
(Find out about the Western Australian shrubland, its wildlife, and how to visit it.)
California State Parks: cal-parks.ca.gov/parkindex/
(Profiles of the areas of shrubland set aside for protection by the California state government.)
Introduction to South Africa's fynbos shrubland: www.botany.uwc.ac.za/envfacts/fynbos/
(A colorful introduction to the region and the plants and animals that live there.)

Index

Page numbers in italics refer to picture captions.

Picture Credits